PHOTOSHOP CS2

ROBERT SHUFFLEBOTHAM

in
easy steps

In easy steps is an imprint of Computer Step
Southfield Road · Southam
Warwickshire CV47 0FB · United Kingdom
www.ineasysteps.com

Notice of Liability
Every effort has been made to ensure that this book contains accurate and
current information. However, Computer Step and the author shall not be
liable for any loss or damage suffered by readers as a result of any information
contained herein.

Trademarks
Photoshop® is a registered trademark of Adobe Systems Incorporated.
All other trademarks are acknowledged as belonging to their respective
companies.

Printed and bound in the United Kingdom

ISBN 1-84078-300-1

Table of Contents

Basic Theory

An understanding of the basics of color is important if you are to get the best out of Photoshop. Refer back to this section from time to time. As your understanding of Photoshop grows, so will your appreciation of the concepts of color that underpin the whole process of image capture and image manipulation.

This chapter also covers RGB and CMYK color models as well as monitor calibration.

Covers

Chapter One

Bitmaps and Vectors

Photoshop is an image-editing application with a wealth of tools and commands for working on digital images or bitmaps. There are utilities for retouching, color correcting, compositing and more. There are also over 90 functional and creative filters that can be applied to entire images, or selected areas within images.

A bitmap image consists of a rectangular grid, or raster, of pixels – in concept, very much like a mosaic. When you edit a bitmap you are editing the color values of individual pixels or groups of pixels.

Image-editing applications differ fundamentally from vector-based applications such as Adobe Illustrator and Macromedia FreeHand. In these applications, you work with objects that can be moved, scaled, transformed, stacked and deleted as individual or grouped objects, but all the time each exists as a complete, separate object.

These applications are called vector drawing packages, as each object is defined by a mathematical formula. Because of this, they are resolution-independent – you can scale vector drawings up or down (either in the originating application or in a page layout application such as QuarkXPress or Adobe InDesign) and they will still print smoothly and crisply.

Scaled to 400%

You should always try to scan an image at, or slightly larger than, the size at which you intend to use it. This means you will avoid having to increase the size of the image.

Vector drawing at actual size

In contrast, bitmaps are created at a set resolution – a fixed number of pixels per inch. If you scan an image at a specific resolution, then double its size, you are effectively halving its resolution (unless you add more pixels). You are likely to end up with a blocky, jagged image, as you have increased the size of the individual pixels that make up the bitmap image.

Scaled to 400%

200 ppi bitmap at
actual size

More, rather than less, color information is usually desirable, as this means the image can represent more shades of color, with finer transitions between colors and greater density of color, leading to a more realistic image.

Photoshop can handle images that use 16-bits per channel that originate from high-end digital cameras and scanners. 16-bit per channel images contain a far greater range of colors than 8-bit per channel images. The disadvantage of working with such images is that their file sizes are also dramatically larger. The bit depth per channel of an image appears in the title bar of the image window:

Waterfall(16bit).tif @ 66.7% (RGB/16)

Bitmaps and bit-depth

An important factor when the digital data for an image is captured, typically at the scanning stage, is its bit-depth. Bit-depth refers to the amount of digital storage space used to record information about the color of a pixel. The more bits you use, the more color information you can store to describe the color of a pixel – but also, the larger the file size you end up with.

To output realistic images using PostScript technology an image should be able to represent 256 gray levels. A 24-bit scan is sufficient for recording 256 gray levels for each of the Red, Green and Blue channels (8-bits for each channel), resulting in a possible combination of over 16 million colors.

Ideally, when you work on images in Photoshop you will do so using a monitor capable of displaying over 16 million colors. This ensures that you see all the color detail in the image. Although you can work on images using only thousands of colors, for best results, especially where color reproduction is important, you need to work with as many colors as possible.

Pixels and Resolution

Pixels

A pixel is the smallest element in a bitmap image captured by a digital camera or a scanner. Pixel is short for "picture element". Zoom in on an image in Photoshop and you will start to see the individual pixels – the fundamental building blocks – that make up the image. When working in Photoshop, you are editing pixels, changing their color, shade and brightness.

Resolution

A key factor when working on bitmap images is resolution. This is measured in pixels per inch (ppi).

Pixels can vary in size. If you have an image with a resolution of 100 ppi, each pixel would be 1/100th of an inch square. In an image with a resolution of 300 ppi, each pixel would be 1/300th of an inch square – giving a much finer, less blocky result.

Printer resolution measured in dots per inch (dpi) is not the same as image resolution measured in pixels per inch (ppi). Printer dots are a fixed size, pixels can vary in size.

When working on images that will eventually be printed on a printing press, you need to work on high-resolution images. These are images whose resolution is twice the halftone screen frequency (measured in lines per inch – lpi) that will be used for final output – that is when you output to bromide, film, or directly to plate.

For example, for a final output screen frequency of 150 lpi – a typical screen frequency used for glossy magazines – you need to capture your image at a resolution of 300 ppi.

Resolutions of double the screen frequency are important for images with fine lines, repeating patterns or textures. You can achieve acceptable results, especially when printing at screen frequencies greater than 133 lpi, using resolutions of 1½ times the final screen frequency.

Images intended for multimedia presentations or the World Wide Web need only be 72 ppi, which is effectively the screen resolution.

To work with images for positional purposes only, as long as you can get accurate enough on-screen results and laser proofs, you can work with much lower resolutions.

RGB and CMYK Color Models

You need to be aware of two color models as you start working with Adobe Photoshop. These are the RGB (Red, Green, Blue) and CMYK (Cyan, Magenta, Yellow and blacK) color models.

RGB is important because it mirrors the way the human eye perceives color. It is the model used by scanners and digital cameras to capture color information in digital format, and it is the way that your computer monitor describes color.

Red, green and blue are referred to as the "additive primaries". You can add varying proportions of the three colors to produce millions of different colors – but still a more limited range (or "gamut") than in nature, due to the limitations of the monitor. If you add 100% red, green and blue light together, you get white. You produce the "secondary" colors when you add red and blue to get magenta; green and blue to get cyan; red and green to get yellow.

On the printing press, cyan, magenta, yellow and black combine to simulate a huge variety of colors. Printers add black because, although in theory, if you combine 100% each of cyan, magenta and yellow you produce black, in reality, because of impurities in the dyes, you only get a muddy brown.

The CMYK color model is referred to as the "subtractive" color model. It is important because this is the color model used by printing presses. If you subtract all cyan, magenta and yellow when printing you end up with the complete absence of color – white.

Color gamuts

Color gamut refers to the range of colors that a specific device is capable of producing. There are millions of colors in the visible spectrum that the eye can discern. Scanners, monitors and printing presses cannot reproduce every color in the visible spectrum – the range of colors they are capable of producing is their gamut.

From the desktop publishing point of view, the process of capturing digital color information, viewing and manipulating this on-screen and then finally printing the image using colored inks is complicated, because the gamut of a color monitor is different to the gamut of CMYK and PANTONE inks. There are colors (especially vibrant yellows and deep blues) that can be displayed on a monitor but cannot be printed using traditional CMYK inks.

Typically you will work in RGB mode if the image is intended for use on the World Wide Web or in a multimedia presentation. You can work in CMYK or RGB mode if the image is intended for print, but you must remember to convert to CMYK mode before saving/exporting in EPS or TIFF file format in order to use the image in a page layout application such as QuarkXPress. Adobe InDesign can import CMYK or RGB images in native Photoshop (.PSD) file format.

When you convert from RGB to CMYK mode, Photoshop converts out-of-gamut colors (in this case, colors that can be seen on screen, but not printed) into their nearest printable equivalent.

The CIE (Commission Internationale de l'Eclairage) Yxy color model is a model that defines the visible spectrum which can be seen by a "standard" observer.

Colors with the same lightness value fall within an approximately triangular flat plane (the Visible Spectrum area in the diagram opposite.) The x axis represents the amount of red in colors and the y axis indicates the amount of green. The Y axis represents the lightness of colors.

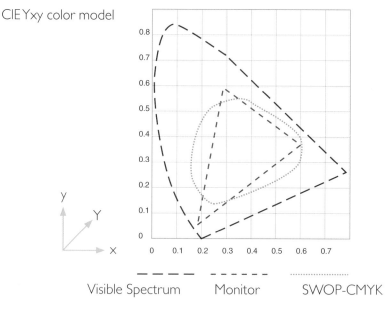

CIE Yxy color model

Visible Spectrum — Monitor — SWOP-CMYK

Color Management

No two devices that represent color, from digital camera to scanner to monitor to printer, will reproduce color in exactly the same way. The aim of a color management system is to ensure, as far as possible, that the colors you see on your screen are as close as possible to the colors you see in the finished work, whether in print or on screen.

Color management settings are available so that you can choose a color management workflow most suitable for your needs.

Using the Color Settings dialog box you can define how you manage color in your images as you work in Photoshop.

1   To specify color management settings for your Photoshop working environment, launch Photoshop, then choose Edit>Color Settings (Ctrl/Command+Shift+K).

2   Choose the most appropriate setting for your intended final output from the Settings pop-up list. For example, if you are using Photoshop for images that will be used in multimedia presentations, or on the World Wide Web, choose Web/Internet or Monitor Color options. If you are working with images that will be color separated then printed using CMYK inks, choose Europe or US Prepress defaults as appropriate.

Europe Prepress 2	⌄
Custom	
Other	
Europe General Purpose 2	
Europe Prepress 2	
Europe Web/Internet	
Monitor Color	

3   Only make changes to the default settings when you have gained experience of using Photoshop and you have a valid reason for making changes, or if you have consulted with your commercial printer and they have suggested changes to suit your specific output requirements.

4 To get a better understanding of how the settings work in the Color Settings dialog box, roll your cursor over the pop-up lists. The Description area at the bottom of the palette updates with information on how the option affects the image.

If you feel that you are not achieving good color in printed output, consult your commercial printer about creating custom settings for color management.

Color Settings

For more information on color settings, search for "setting up color management" in Help. This term is searchable from any Creative Suite application.

Settings: Europe Prepress 2

Working Spaces

RGB: Adobe RGB (1998)

CMYK: Europe ISO Coated FOGRA27

Gray: Dot Gain 15%

Spot: Dot Gain 15%

Color Management Policies

RGB: Preserve Embedded Profiles

CMYK: Preserve Embedded Profiles

Gray: Preserve Embedded Profiles

Profile Mismatches: ☑ Ask When Opening ☑ Ask When Pasting

Missing Profiles: ☑ Ask When Opening

Description

Europe Prepress 2: Preparation of content for common printing conditions in Europe. CMYK values are preserved. Profile warnings are enabled.

OK
Reset
Load...
Save...
More Options
☑ Preview

A CMS (Color Management System) is used to translate colors accurately from one color device to another. It attempts to represent a color consistently from the color space in which the image was created to the color space used at output, making adjustments so that color displays as consistently as possible across a range of monitors and other devices.

5 Click the More Options button to access advanced color management settings. Only change advanced settings if you have a detailed understanding of color management.

Monitor Calibration

It is important to calibrate your monitor so that colors in your image are displayed accurately. Calibrating your monitor should eliminate any color casts (typically reddish or blueish) on your monitor and ensure that the monitor displays grays as neutrally as possible.

Calibrate the monitor you are using in order to define the RGB color space that your monitor can display. Once you have calibrated your monitor, Photoshop can compensate for the differences between the color space in which your image resides and the color space of the monitor you are using.

Windows users can use the Adobe Gamma utility to calibrate the contrast and brightness, gamma (midtones), color balance and the white point of the monitor. Use the Adobe Gamma Wizard if you do not have previous experience of calibrating a monitor. For the Macintosh, use the Calibrate utility found in System Preferences>Displays.

Calibration settings that you create are saved as an ICC (International Color Consortium) profile with an .icm extension.

Hardware-based color calibration utilities are more accurate than the Adobe Gamma utility. You should use only one calibration utility. Colors may appear incorrectly if you use more than one utility.

1 (Macintosh) Choose Apple Menu>System Preferences>Displays. Click the Color tab. Click the Calibrate button, then follow the on-screen prompts.

The easiest way to locate the Adobe Gamma utility in Windows XP is to choose Start>Settings>Control Panel, then click the Switch to Classic view option in the sidebar on the left of the window.

2 (Windows) Choose Control Panel from the Start Menu. Double-click the Adobe Gamma icon to display the dialog box. Choose Step by Step (Wizard), then click the Next button.

3 Click the Load button to choose a monitor profile which matches the monitor you are using most closely. (Windows) Profiles are stored in the Windows\System32\spool\ drivers\color folder. (Mac) Profiles are stored in the System/Library/ColorSync/Profiles folder.

Profiles should be available from your monitor manufacturer's website.

Leave your monitor turned on for at least 30 minutes before you calibrate. This allows the phosphors time to warm up fully and the display to stabilize.

4 Adjust the Brightness and Contrast settings of your monitor. Refer to the monitor handbook if you are unsure of how to adjust these settings. Click the Next button.

5 Only change the Phosphors pop-up if you know that your monitor's phosphors are

different from the default selection. Click the Next button.

Defocus your eyes slightly to help achieve the correct setting for the View Single Gamma slider.

6 With the View Single Gamma Only option selected, drag the Gamma slider until the square in the middle of the patterned lines fades, as far as possible, into the pattern. This defines the brightness of the midtones on

your monitor. Click the Next button. For Desired Gamma choose a target gamma. This option is not available on Windows systems which cannot control the monitor. For images intended for the World Wide Web or multimedia presentations, choose a gamma of 2.2. If you intend to print images using CMYK inks, you should typically choose a gamma of 1.8. Click the Next button.

For monitor calibration to be effective, you should not adjust the brightness and contrast settings on your monitor after you have completed the calibration process, and you must ensure that the lighting conditions within the room remain constant.

7 Leave the Hardware White Point on the default setting unless you

know this to be inaccurate. Click Next. Leave Adjusted White Point on Same as Hardware unless you want to view the image at a different color temperature to that set by the monitor's factory-specified setting. Click the Next button.

Recalibrate your monitor on a regular basis, as monitor performance can change over time.

8 Click the Finish button to save settings as an .icm compatible profile. Name the profile and save it to the ColorSync Profiles folder.

The Working Environment

This section covers the basics of the Photoshop working environment, getting you used to the Photoshop window, the Toolbox, palettes and a number of standard Photoshop conventions and techniques that you will find useful as you develop your Photoshop skills.

It also covers the basics of printing composite images to a color inkjet printer as well as techniques for undoing commands as you work on your images.

Covers

Chapter Two

The Photoshop Screen Environment

There are three "screen modes" to choose from when working on images in Photoshop. The screen mode icons are located at the bottom of the toolbox.

Full Screen with Menu Bar mode is useful when working on individual images because it clears away the clutter of the Finder environment (Mac), or the Windows desktop. Use Full Screen mode to see the image without the distraction of other screen elements, and without any other colors interfering with the colors in your image.

Standard Screen Mode

Full Screen with Menu Bar mode

Full Screen mode

1 Click this icon to return to Standard Screen mode.

2 Click this icon to go to Full Screen with Menu Bar mode.

3 Click this icon to go to Full Screen mode. Press the Tab key to hide/show the Toolbox and palettes.

4 Click the Edit in ImageReady button to launch ImageReady. (See page 206).

Command (often referred to as "Apple" on the Mac) and Ctrl (Windows), and Alt/option (Mac) and Alt (Windows) are used identically as modifier keys. Shift is standard on both platforms.

This book uses Alt, with an uppercase "A" to denote both the Macintosh and Windows key of that name.

Windows users can use the right mouse button to access context sensitive menus; Mac users can hold down the Control key and press their single mouse button.

Every time you launch Photoshop the Welcome screen appears. Click on one of the listed links, or click the Close button to start working with Photoshop. To prevent the Welcome screen appearing the next time you launch Photoshop, deselect the Show this dialog at startup option.

Windows environment

The Windows environment offers identical functionality to the Macintosh environment, as you can see from a comparison of the Windows and Macintosh application window screen shots.

The Image window

Close button

Title bar

Image

Scroll bars

Resize box

View %

Using the Toolbox

There are a number of useful general techniques that relate to choosing tools in the Toolbox, including those from the expanded range of hidden tool pop-ups.

Create your own, custom keyboard shortcuts using Edit>Keyboard Shortcuts. You can either edit the default shortcuts set, or create a new set by clicking the New button. Click on a command in the commands scroll list, enter a keyboard shortcut combination in the shortcut entry area that appears to the right, then click the Add Shortcut button. Click OK when you finish creating shortcuts

Set Foreground color

Default colors (D)

Edit in Standard mode

Standard Screen mode (F)

Switch colors (X)

Set Background color

Edit in Quick Mask mode

Full Screen mode (F)

Full Screen mode with Menu Bar (F)

Edit in ImageReady

Double-click on a tool to show the Options bar for that tool if it is not already showing.

1   Press the keyboard shortcut (in brackets) to access tools.

2   Click and hold on any tool with a small triangle in the bottom right corner to see all tools in that tool group.

When you select a tool in the Toolbox, the Options bar, extending across the top of the Photoshop window, updates according to the tool you select. Get into the habit of checking the settings in the Options bar before you proceed to use the tool.

3   Hold down Alt/option and click on any tool in a tool group to cycle through the available tools. Alternatively, hold down Shift, then press the keyboard shortcut for that tool group a number of times. For example, press "O" three times to cycle through all the tools in the Dodge tool group.

4   Press Tab to hide/show all palettes, including the toolbox. Hold down Shift, then press the Tab key to hide/show all palettes except the Toolbox.

Use Display & Cursor Preferences in the Edit>Preferences menu to change the default appearance of painting and other cursors.

5   Press Caps Lock to change the painting or brush size cursor to a precise crosshair cursor, which indicates the center of the painting tool. Press Caps Lock again to return to the standard cursor display.

Document and Scratch Sizes

The Sizes bar is useful for monitoring disk space and memory considerations as you work on your images.

Document Sizes

*Choose Edit>
Preferences>
Plug-Ins & Scratch
Disks (Windows),
or Photoshop>
Preferences>Plug-Ins & Scratch
Disks (Mac) to specify the hard
disk(s) you want Photoshop to
use as a Scratch disk. Ideally, the
primary Scratch disk should be
your fastest hard drive.*

With Document Sizes selected, you see two numbers separated by a

slash. The first number is the size of the image with all layers flattened. The second number may be larger and represents the file storage size whilst the image contains additional layers and/or alpha channels you may have set up. In images that consist of only a single layer, with no additional channels, both numbers are the same.

Scratch Sizes

The Scratch disk is an underlying technical detail that you should be aware of when using Photoshop. The Scratch disk is a designated hard disk that Photoshop utilizes as "virtual" memory if it runs out of memory (RAM) whilst working on one or more images.

*To improve
performance
when working
with large image
files, a Scratch
disk should be on a different drive
than the one where the image
is located.*

With Scratch Sizes selected in the Sizes Bar you again see two numbers separated by a slash. The first number represents the amount of memory (RAM) Photoshop needs to handle all currently open pictures. The second number represents the actual amount of memory available to Photoshop. When the first number is greater than the second, Photoshop is using the Scratch disk as virtual memory.

As a general rule of thumb when working in Photoshop, you should have free disk space of at least 3-5 times the file size of the image you are working on. This is because Photoshop makes use of the Scratch disk as virtual memory and because Photoshop needs to hold more than one copy of the image you are working on for the Undo, Revert and History palette functions.

Ruler Guides and Grids

Make sure you select View>Snap To>Guides/Grid, if you want cursors and selections to snap to guides and the grid. These options are very useful for aligning elements accurately.

You can show a grid in your image window to help with alignment and measuring, and you can also drag in ruler guides. Both sets of guides are non-printing. Customize the appearance of the grid and guides using Edit>Preferences>Guides, Grid & Slices (Windows), Photoshop>Preferences>Guides, Grid & Slices (Mac).

1 To show or hide the grid, choose View>Show/Hide Grid.

Use keyboard shortcuts: Ctrl/Command+; to Hide/Show ruler guides; Ctrl/Command+' to Hide/Show the grid.

2 To create a ruler guide, first choose View>Rulers to display the rulers along the top and left edges of the image window. Position your cursor in a ruler and then click and drag onto your image to create either a vertical or horizontal guide.

Take care when repositioning ruler guides that you don't reposition an entire layer accidentally. Make sure you see the bi-directional arrows which indicate that you are dragging a guide.

3 To reposition a ruler guide, select the Move tool, position your cursor on a guide, then click and drag. The cursor changes to a bi-directional arrow when you pick up a guide. To remove a ruler guide, drag the ruler guide back into the ruler it came from. Alternatively, choose View>Clear Guides to remove all guides.

4 To temporarily hide any grid or guides in order to preview the image without the clutter of non-printing guides, choose View> Extras (Ctrl/Command+H). Use the same command to bring back the guides and grid.

Moving Around

Use any combination of the Navigator palette, the Zoom tool, the Hand tool and the scroll bars for moving around and zooming in and out of your image.

1   Choose Window>Show Navigator to show the Navigator palette. In the palette, you can double-click the % entry box, enter a zoom % (0.20 – 1600%), then press Return/Enter. Alternatively, drag the zoom slider to the right to zoom in, or to the left to zoom out. Each time you change your zoom level, the view in the Preview area updates.

Hold down Ctrl/Command and the Spacebar to temporarily access the Zoom tool with any other tool selected. Add the Alt/option key to the above combination to zoom out.

2   Drag the red View box in the Preview area to move quickly to different areas of your image.

3   To use the Zoom tool, select it, position your cursor on the image and click to zoom in on the area around your cursor, in preset increments. With the Zoom tool selected, hold down Alt/option. The cursor changes to the zoom out cursor; click to zoom out in the preset increments.

With any other tool selected, hold down the Spacebar to temporarily access the Hand tool.

4   With the Zoom tool selected, you can also click and drag to define the area you want to zoom in on.

5   You can use the Hand tool in addition to using the scroll bars to move around your image when you have zoomed in on it. Select the tool, position your cursor on the image, then click and drag to reposition.

The Info Palette

The Info palette (Window>Info) provides useful numerical read-outs relative to the position of the cursor on your image.

You can use it as an on-screen densitometer to examine color values at the cursor. There are two color read-outs. As a default, the first color read-out is the actual color under the cursor. For example, a read-out of red, green, and blue color components in an RGB image. The default second read-out is for cyan, magenta, yellow and black values.

The palette also displays x and y coordinates, giving the precise location of the cursor as it moves over the image.

If you create a selection, there is a read-out of the width and height of the selection. The palette also displays values for some options such as rotating, skewing and scaling selections.

An exclamation mark next to the CMYK readouts indicates that a color is outside the printable CMYK gamut or range of colors:

C :	87!
M :	0!
Y :	21!
K :	0!
8-bit	

1 To change the default settings for the Info Palette, choose Palette Options from the Info palette menu.

2 Use the Mode pop-ups to choose the first and second color read-outs.

3 You can also choose a unit of measurement for mouse coordinates.

Palette Techniques

This page uses Macintosh and Windows screen shots to illustrate the degree of similarity in functionality between the Windows and Macintosh platforms.

There are seventeen floating palettes in Photoshop, (not including the Toolbox or the Options bar). These movable palettes appear in front of images. Initially the palettes are grouped together.

1   You can show any of the palette groups by selecting the appropriate palette from the Window menu. To close a palette, click on the Close button (Mac) or Close icon (Windows) in the title bar of each palette.

2   To move a palette, simply position your cursor in the title bar, then click and drag.

Choose Window> Workspace> Reset palette locations to recreate the default arrangement of Photoshop's palettes.

3   To choose a particular palette, click on the appropriate tab just below the title bar. You can drag these tabs to create separate palettes. Alternatively, you can drag a tab into another palette to create your own custom groupings of palettes.

4   You can shrink or roll up palettes to make the most of your available screen space. Click the Zoom box (Mac) or Minimize icon (Windows) in the title bar of the palette. Repeat the procedure to restore the palette to its original size. (You have to click twice on the Zoom/Minimize icon if the palette has been resized.)

Double-click a palette tab to collapse the palette to its tab and title bar only. Double-click the tab again to restore it to its previous size.

...cont'd

Press the Tab key to hide/show all palettes including the Toolbox. Hold down Shift, then press Tab to hide/show currently visible palettes, with the exception of the Toolbox.

5 Use standard Macintosh and Windows techniques to resize the Swatches, Navigator, Layers, Channels, Actions, Styles and Paths palettes by dragging.

6 With a painting or editing tool selected, to restore the default settings for all tools, click the pop-up triangle for the Tool Presets palette, then click the palette menu triangle (⊙). Choose Reset All Tools from the pop-up menu.

7 All palettes have a palette menu for accessing a range of commands or options relevant to the palette. Click the triangle to access the palette menu.

Choose Window> Workspace>Save Workspace to save the current position of your palettes. Enter a name for this workspace arrangement in the Save Workspace dialog box. Choose Window>Workspace then select the name of the workspace to reset palettes to this arrangement.

8 At screen resolutions greater than 800x600, the Options bar has a palette docking area on the right-hand side. Drag a palette tab into the docking area to create a drop-down palette. Click on the palette tab to access the palette. Click on the triangle in the palette tab to access the palette menu for the palette. After making changes to settings

in a palette, it collapses back into the docking well when you perform another action on the image. Drag the palette out of the docking well to revert the palette to a standard floating palette.

2. The Working Environment   27

Saving and Loading Custom Settings

When you save settings, you create an independent settings file which stores the custom information. You can load these settings into other images as necessary.

The Swatches, Styles and Actions palettes, the Brushes presets, along with dialog boxes such as Duotones, Levels and Curves, have Save and Load options which allow you to save custom settings made in the palette or dialog box and then load them into the same image, or into other Photoshop images, when required. The following example uses the Swatches palette.

It's a good idea to set up a folder within your Adobe folder, or any other appropriate location, for saving your own custom settings. This means you can access and load the settings quickly and conveniently whenever you need them.

1   After creating a custom Swatches palette (see Chapter 4), choose Save Swatches in the palette menu (in a dialog box, click the Save button).

Look in the Presets folder, within the Photoshop CS2 folder, for brush presets that come with Photoshop. Try the Assorted Brushes folder as a starting point for experimenting with different brush types.

2   The Save dialog box prompts you for a file name and location in which to save the settings. The default Color Swatches folder is in the Presets folder within the Photoshop CS2 folder. The extension for a Color Swatches file is .aco. Make sure you save the file with the correct extension.

Choose Reset Swatches in the palette menu to restore settings to their original defaults.

3   To load previously saved settings, choose Replace Swatches or Load Swatches in the palette menu (in a dialog box click the Load button), then specify the location of the settings you previously saved. Click on the name, then click Open. Load Swatches adds the new swatches to the existing swatches in the palette. Replace Swatches replaces the current swatches with the new set.

Printing

The appearance of the Page Setup dialog box varies according to the printer selected. Non-PostScript printers do not offer a complete set of options.

When you have made all the necessary edits and adjustments to an image you are ready to print. You can print using the standard Print dialog box, or you can use the Print with Preview command to access additional print features and a preview of the image as it will print on the specified paper size.

1 Choose File>Print. Make sure the correct printer is selected from the Name pop-up menu. Enter the number of copies you want to print. Some options are available only if you are printing to a PostScript printer.

In the Print with Preview dialog box, click the More Options button, then choose Output from the drop down menu if you want to specify additional printed information such as Crop Marks and Calibration bars. As you switch on the various options they appear in the preview area:

2 Click the Properties button in the Print dialog box to set controls specific to your printer. In particular, make sure the Paper Type and Size are set correctly, check that the orientation is appropriate and select a quality option. Refer to the manufacturer's manual for information on the options available for the printer. Click OK.

3 OK the Print dialog box to print a copy of the image.

Print with Preview

1 Choose File>Print with Preview to see a representation of the image as it will print on the specified paper size.

In the expanded Print with Preview dialog box, only change Color Management options if you are not satisfied with your printed output. In some cases, choosing Let Photoshop Determine Colors from the Color Handling pop-up can produce improved color output.

2 If necessary, click the Scale to Fit Media checkbox to reduce the size of the image so that it fits onto the specified paper size. Click the Page Setup button to access printer specific controls. Click the Print button when you are ready to print.

Picture Package

The Picture Package command enables you to print multiple copies of an image, at various sizes, on a single sheet of paper.

1   To create a Picture Package, choose File>Automate>Picture Package. Select the image you want to use from the Use pop-up menu.

Click the Edit Layout button in the bottom of the Layout area to manually arrange the images in your picture package:

Edit Layout...

2   From the Document area, choose the page size you want to print onto. Then choose a layout arrangement from the Layout pop-up. The Layout area on the right updates to indicate the positioning of the images. Specify Resolution and Color Mode options.

3   Use the Content pop-up to choose a label type if required. Select Custom Text to enter details in the Custom Text field. Control the appearance and position of text labels using the other controls.

4   When you OK the dialog box, Photoshop prepares the multiple copies of the image as a single picture package file which you can print or save.

The History Palette

Every time you modify your image Photoshop records this as a new state in the History palette. The History palette records the last 20 states of the image. Use the History palette to return to a previous state of the image within the current work session. The most recent state of the image appears at the bottom of the list in the palette.

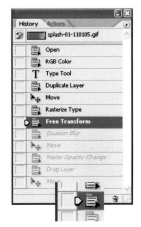

1. To return to a previous state of the image, click on a state in the History palette. The image reverts to that stage of the work session. States after the state you click on are dimmed. These subsequent states are discarded if you continue to work from the selected state.

2. Alternatively, drag the state slider up or down to indicate the state you wish to move to. Or, choose Step Forward/Step Backward from the palette menu (▶), to move sequentially through the states.

Deleting states

You can delete states from the History palette to remove the changes to the image recorded by that state and all subsequent states.

1. To delete a history state, click on its name, then choose Delete from the palette menu. Alternatively, drag the state into the Wastebasket icon at the bottom of the palette.

Dock to Palette Well	
Step Forward	Shift+Ctrl+Z
Step Backward	Alt+Ctrl+Z
New Snapshot...	
Delete	
Clear History	
New Document	
History Options...	

Clearing states

Clearing states leaves the image at its current state, but removes all previous states from the History palette.

1. To clear the History palette, use the palette menu to choose Clear History. All recorded states are deleted from the History palette, leaving the image at its most recent state.

Purging states

Purging states is useful if you get a low memory message. This is typically because the Undo buffer is becoming full with the changes to the image that it is having to record. When you purge states they are deleted from the Undo buffer, freeing up memory.

To purge states, hold down Alt/option, then choose Clear History from the palette menu in the History palette. This command purges history states from the active image. Choose Edit>Purge Histories if you want to purge all history states for all open images.

You cannot undo
the Purge states
commands.

Snapshots

An initial "snapshot" is created by default when you open an image. This appears at the top of the History palette. As you work on the image, the History palette records the results of the last 20 operations performed. Older states of the image are automatically deleted to keep memory free for Photoshop. You can keep particular states of an image during a work session by making additional snapshots.

Snapshots record
the state of
an image at a
particular point
in time. They
are useful if you want to retain
a particular state of the image
so that you can return to it at a
later stage.

To create additional snapshots, click on any state in the History palette. Choose New Snapshot from the palette menu. In the New Snapshot dialog box enter a name. OK the dialog box. A new snapshot is added in the top section of the History palette.

Click on a snapshot to revert to the state of the image when the snapshot was created. If you select a snapshot, then continue to work on the image, all history states are lost.

Snapshots exist
for the current
work session only.
When you close
an image, all
snapshots are lost.

To delete a snapshot, click once on the snapshot to select it, then click on the Wastebasket icon at the bottom of the palette.

Opening and Saving Files

Adobe Photoshop began life with the primary purpose of converting image formats for use in different applications and on different platforms. Since then it has gone on to become a market-leading image-editing application. This chapter covers the basic techniques of opening and saving images in Photoshop.

Covers

Chapter Three

Opening Images in Photoshop

After you launch Photoshop you can open images using the File menu. The Adobe Bridge provides a powerful and flexible alternative method for locating and opening images (see page 38 for further information).

(see page 38 for further information)

1   To open a picture from within Photoshop, choose File>Open. This takes you into the Open dialog box. Navigate through folders and sub-folders as necessary to locate the file you wish to open, click on the file name to select it, then click Open. Alternatively, just double-click the file name.

Double-click Photoshop file icons in the Windows or Macintosh file-management environments to open the file. If Photoshop is not running, this also launches Photoshop.

2   Select the Show All Readable Documents (Mac), or choose All Formats from the Files of type pop-up (Windows), to show all files in the selected folder.

3   You can also open recently opened files by choosing File>Open Recent. Select a file from the list.

Choose Edit> Preferences>File Handling (Windows), or, Photoshop Preferences>File Handling (Mac), then enter a number for Recent file list contains to control the number of files that appear in the Recent files sub-menu:

`Recent file list contains: 10 files`

4   (Mac) To search for a file that you want to open from within the Open dialog box, click the Find button. Enter the file name, then click Find/Find Again, until you find the file.

Scanning into Photoshop

You can scan into Photoshop using the File>Import sub menu. Make sure you install the scanning software for your scanner before you begin.

| To create a scan from within Photoshop, choose File>Import, then select the appropriate scanner from the sub-menu.

Typically, you can either scan using the scanner's default settings, or you can customize settings including: scan mode (grayscale, color, line art etc.), resolution, scale, contrast, brightness and gamma. Refer to your scanning software manual for details of the controls available.

Many of the scanning controls have equivalent functions in Photoshop. Scanning options vary from scanner to scanner, but you should be able to specify whether you are scanning a transparency or a photograph. The other essential decisions you need to make at this stage are image mode, resolution and scale. You will also need to specify a crop area in the preview window.

For WIA compliant scanners, choose File>Import>WIA Support. In the WIA Support dialog box click the Browse button to specify a location in which to save the scanned image, then click the Start button. Select your scanner in the Select Device dialog box. Click OK to begin the scan. Select scanner specific options as necessary. Refer to the manufacturer's manual for detailed information on the options available.

2 Click the Scan button. Wait until the scanning process finishes and the image appears in an untitled Photoshop window. Save the image.

Opening and Placing EPS files

EPS stands for Encapsulated Postscript. EPS files can contain bitmap as well as vector information. EPS files, created in applications such as Adobe Illustrator and Macromedia FreeHand, typically contain object-oriented or "vector" format information.

Opening an Illustrator EPS file

When you open an EPS file in Photoshop, it is rasterized: that is, the vector information is converted into Photoshop's pixel-based format.

1   To open an EPS file as a new document, choose File>Open. Locate and highlight the EPS file you want to open, then click the Open button. Alternatively, double-click the file name.

2   In the Rasterize dialog box, choose a unit of measurement from the pop-up menus next to the Height and Width fields, and enter new dimensions if required. Enter the resolution required for your final output device and choose an image mode from the Mode pop-up menu.

3   Select the Constrain Proportions box to keep the original proportions of the EPS. Select Anti-aliased to slightly blur pixels along edges to avoid unwanted jagged edges. Click OK. The EPS appears in its own image window. It is now a bitmap image.

Placing an Illustrator EPS file

You can also "place" an Illustrator or FreeHand EPS file into an open Photoshop document. The placed artwork typically appears on a new Smart Objects layer.

Before you accept the placed EPS, you can also use the Options bar to change position, size, rotation and skew values numerically for the file.

To place an EPS file into an existing Photoshop file, first open an image in Photoshop, or create a new document.

...cont'd

To create anti-aliased edges for a placed EPS, you must select the Anti-aliased option in the Options bar before you click the Accept button.

If you don't want to accept the placed image, with the bounding box still visible press the Esc key. If you have already placed the image you will have to delete the new layer. (See page 108.)

You can copy vector artwork from Illustrator into Photoshop using the clipboard.

In Illustrator, copy selected artwork using Edit>Copy, then, in Photoshop, choose Edit>Paste. Choose Path in the Paste dialog box to import the artwork as paths in the Paths palette:

2 Choose File>Place. Use the Place dialog box to specify the location and name of the EPS file, then click the Place button.

3 The Place PDF dialog box appears. Leave the Select pop-up menu set to Page. In the Options area, use the Crop To pop-up to specify the area of the Illustrator file you want to import. Click OK.

4 A bounding box with eight "handles" and a cross through the placed image appears in the Photoshop image window. The EPS image itself may take a few seconds to draw inside the bounding box.

5 If necessary, drag a corner handle to resize the placed image. Hold down Shift as you drag to maintain proportions. Position your cursor inside the bounding box of the placed image and drag to reposition the image.

6 When you are satisfied, press Return/Enter; double-click inside the bounding box, or click the Commit button in the Options bar. The rasterized file is placed on a new Smart Objects layer.

Adobe Bridge

Click the Favorites tab, then click Bridge Center to display the main Adobe Bridge window if necessary.

Adobe Bridge acts as a control center, providing cross-product integration, allowing you to locate, track, and organize files and digital assets from a wide variety of sources. Click the Go to Bridge button in the Options bar to launch Adobe Bridge from within Photoshop.

1 Click the Adobe Stock Photos panel to search online for images from stock photo libraries. A search area opens where you can enter keywords or Image IDs to begin your search.

You can launch Adobe Bridge as a standalone application, as you would launch any other application – from the Start>Programs menu in Windows, or from the Applications folder on the Mac.

2 The Recent Folders pane lists the most recent folders used by Creative Suite applications on your computer. Click a folder icon to display the contents.

To create a file group, make sure only files you want to include are open in their respective applications. Click the Save open files into a file group option. In the Adobe Bridge dialog box, enter a name for the file group. OK the dialog box:

3 The Recent Files pane lists the most recent files used by applications on your computer. Click a file icon to open the file. If the appropriate application is not running, Bridge launches it and opens the file so that you can work on it.

To open a project of related files previously saved as a file group, click the file group folder icon in the list then click in the Open this file group panel.

4 If you are working with files in different applications which are part of the same project, and the files are currently open, you can use Adobe Bridge to create a file group. This brings together the related files and makes it easy to manage, locate and track all the related files in a project.

Folders/File Browser View

Click the Folders tab to view, manage, sort and open images on your hard disk. You can also use the Folder view to create new folders and to rename, move, delete and rank image files.

Choose an option from the View>Sort sub-menu to control the way image thumbnails are ordered in the Preview pane:

Ascending Order

✔ By Filename
By Document Kind
By Date Created
By Date File Modified
By File Size
By Dimensions
By Resolution
By Label
By Rating
By Version Cue Status

Manually

To move a file, position your cursor on the image thumbnail, then drag it to a different folder in the Folder panel of the Adobe Bridge window. To copy a file to a new location, hold down Alt/option, then drag it to a different folder.

1 In the Adobe Bridge window, click the Folder tab. Use the Folder panel to navigate to specific folders on your hard disk using standard Windows/Macintosh techniques. You can also use the Look in drop down list, to navigate quickly to recently used folders.

2 The content area on the right of the window displays thumbnail previews of the contents of the selected folder.

3 Drag the Thumbnail Size slider to control the size of thumbnail previews in the contents area. Use the View buttons to control their arrangement.

3 File information for a selected image file appears in the Metadata and Keyword palettes. With the Metadata tab selected, click the expand triangle to the left of Camera Data (Exif) to view image information imported from a digital camera.

4 To open a file from the content area, click on an image thumbnail to select it, then press the Enter/Return key. You can also double-click a thumbnail.

5 To delete a file, click on the file thumbnail to select it, then either click the Wastebasket icon in the Toolbar, or drag the file onto the Wastebasket. Alternatively, you can press the Delete key.

6 To create a 1–5 star ranking for an image, click the leftmost dot below the thumbnail to convert it to a star. To remove a star, click the star to the left of the final star.

7 To display only thumbnails with a specific star rating or higher, select an option from the Filter pop-up menu.

8 Click the Metadata or Keywords tab to view additional labeling information saved with an image. You can also use options from the palette menu for each tab to add and edit metadata and keyword information for your image files. Use the Expand/Collapse triangle to display/hide information for each category.

9 To run a slide show for images in a folder, choose View>Slide Show. Use the Adobe Bridge Slide Show panel to control the slide show. Press H on the keyboard to hide or show the Slide Show commands panel

Saving Files

Using the Save and Save As commands in ImageReady always saves a file in Photoshop (.psd) file format.

The basic principles of saving files in Photoshop – using "Save" and "Save As" – are the same as in any other Macintosh or Windows application. Save regularly as you modify an image so that you do not lose any changes you make should a system crash occur. You should use Save As to save a new file in the first instance, to make copies of a file, to save a file to a new location and when you need to save an image in a different file format.

To create a Thumbnail icon that displays in the Thumbnail area of the Open dialog box, choose Edit>Preferences>File Handling (Windows), or Photoshop> Preferences>File Handling (Mac). Select Always Save from the Image Previews pop-up:

Photoshop supports numerous file formats for opening and saving images. Typically, you save an image in a particular format to meet specific output or printing specifications, to compress the image to save disk space, or to open or import the image into an application that requires a particular file format.

1 To save an image in the first instance, choose File>Save As. Specify where you want to save the file. Enter a name for the file. Use the Format pop-up to choose an appropriate format. Click the Save button. File extensions are added automatically.

2 To save changes as you work on an image, choose File>Save. The previously saved file information is updated.

When you save an image with layers in Photoshop format you get an option to Maximize Compatibility. To ensure greatest flexibility using the image in conjunction with other Adobe products it is best to leave this option selected, although this can increase the file size.

Photoshop format
Use this format as you work on your image. Applications such as QuarkXPress cannot import images in Photoshop format, but all Photoshop options, in particular layers, remain available to you in this format. Photoshop also performs open and save routines more quickly when using its native format.

TIFF Format

TIFF (Tagged Image File Format) became a standard file format for scanned images in the early days of desktop publishing. It is common on both Mac and Windows platforms and is compatible with most paint, image-editing and page layout applications.

On the Macintosh, choose Photoshop> Preferences> File Handling to specify whether or not you want file extensions – e.g. ".tif" – automatically added when saving files.

1 To save an image in TIFF format, choose File>Save As. The Save As dialog box appears. Specify where you want to save the image and enter a name in the name entry box. Use the Format pop-up menu to choose TIFF, then click OK.

| File name: | girlsyemen.tif |
| Format: | TIFF (*.TIF,*.TIFF) |

2 The TIFF Options dialog box will appear. Select Byte Order options and LZW Compression as required, then OK the dialog box.

TIFF Options

Image Compression
- ○ NONE
- ⊙ LZW
- ○ ZIP
- ○ JPEG

Quality: [ ] Maximum
small file   large file

Pixel Order
- ⊙ Interleaved (RGBRGB)
- ○ Per Channel (RRGGBB)

Byte Order
- ⊙ IBM PC
- ○ Macintosh

☐ Save Image Pyramid
☐ Save Transparency

Layer Compression
- ○ RLE (faster saves, bigger files)
- ○ ZIP (slower saves, smaller files)
- ○ Discard Layers and Save a Copy

OK   Cancel

Some applications cannot open or import image files saved in TIFF file format with JPEG or Zip compression.

Pixel Order

Earlier versions of Photoshop wrote tiffs with channel order interleaved. Per Channel usually produces better compression. Both are compatible with earlier versions of Photoshop.

A warning appears at the bottom of the Save As dialog box if an image uses features, such as layers or alpha channels, that are not supported by that particular file format. You are prompted to save a copy of the file. Photoshop automatically adds the word "copy" to the file name.

⚠ File must be saved as a copy with this selection.

Byte Order

Use this option to specify whether you want the TIFF to be used on a Mac or a PC, as Mac and PC TIFF formats vary slightly. Most recently released applications can read files using either option.

LZW Compression

(Lempel-Zif-Welch) is a compression format that looks for repeated elements in the computer code that describes the image and replaces these with shorter sequences. It is a "lossless" compression scheme – none of the image's detail is lost. Applications such as QuarkXPress, Adobe InDesign and Macromedia FreeHand can import TIFFs with LZW compression.

Zip

Zip is a lossless compression format and achieves greatest compression in images that contain areas of solid color. Zip compression is supported by PDF and TIFF file formats.

JPEG

JPEG is a "lossy" compression format (see page 45). JPEG compression is most suitable for photographic type images with variations in highlight and shadow detail throughout the image. (See page 197 for further information on choosing quality options for JPEG compression.)

You can save images in CMYK, RGB, Lab, Index Color and Grayscale using TIFF file format.

Save Image Pyramid

Although Photoshop itself cannot work with multiple resolutions in the same file, you can select the Save Image Pyramid option to preserve multiple resolutions already in a file. Some applications (such as Adobe InDesign) provide support for opening multiresolution files.

Save Transparency

For images that contain transparent areas you can select Save Transparency. Transparent areas

☐ Save Image Pyramid
☐ Save Transparency

are saved in an additional Alpha channel for use when the file is opened in a different application. Transparency is always retained when a file is opened in Photoshop.

Layer Compression

Photoshop can read layer information saved in TIFF file format, although most other applications cannot.

Layer Compression
◉ RLE (faster saves, bigger files)
○ ZIP (slower saves, smaller files)
○ Discard Layers and Save a Copy

Files saved with layers are larger than image files that have been flattened into a single layer. Choose Layer Compression options to specify how pixel data in layers is compressed. RLE (Run Length Encoding) is a lossless compression format supported by many Windows file formats. Select Discard Layers and Save a Copy if you do not want to preserve layers in the image.

Photoshop EPS

EPS is generally more reliable for PostScript printing than the TIFF file format, but generates file sizes which can be three to four times greater than TIFFs with LZW compression. To save in EPS format, do the following:

Follow the procedure for saving TIFFs, but choose Photoshop EPS from the Format pop-up menu. Click OK. The EPS Options dialog box appears. Specify your settings, then click OK.

You can save Duotone, CMYK, RGB, Lab, Bitmap and Grayscale images using Photoshop EPS file format.

Preview

This option specifies the quality of the low-resolution screen preview you see when you import the image into applications such as Adobe InDesign and QuarkXPress. Use "Macintosh (8bits/ pixel)" for a color preview. "Macintosh (JPEG)" uses JPEG compression routines, but is only supported by PostScript Level 2 printers. Use TIFF if you want to use the image in Windows.

Photoshop EPS file format does not support alpha channels.

Encoding

Try choosing ASCII or ASCII85 if you experience printing problems or network issues with images saved in Photoshop EPS format.

The encoding option determines how image data is transmitted to the printing device. Use binary encoding if you want to export the image for use with Adobe Illustrator. Binary encoding typically produces a smaller file size. Some applications do not recognize binary encoding; in this case you have to use ASCII. JPEG encoding options discard image data in order to create smaller file sizes.

Select the Include Vector Data checkbox to include vector data such as shapes or type present in the image.

JPEG Format

The JPEG compression routine is a "lossy" procedure. To make the file size of the image smaller, image data is discarded, resulting in reduced image quality. Extreme JPEG compression can result in noticeably reduced image quality.

1. Follow the procedure for saving in TIFF format, but choose JPEG from the Format pop-up menu. OK the Save As dialog box.

2. Use the Quality pop-up to specify the amount of compression, or drag the slider. Maximum gives best image quality, retaining most of the detail in an image, but results in the least compression. Low gives lowest image quality, but gives maximum compression.

3. In the Format Options area, select Baseline Optimized to optimize the color quality of the image.

4. Select Progressive and enter a value for Scans if you intend to use the image on the World Wide Web and want the image to download in a series of passes adding detail progressively.

5. The compressed file size is indicated in the Size area. Choose a modem speed from the Size pop-up to see an estimated download time for the image at the specified modem speed.

Creating a New File

Whilst the New dialog box is active, if you have an image already open, you can choose Window, then click the name of any open image file listed at the bottom of the menu; the New dialog box updates with the settings from the file you selected.

Photoshop creates a new file with square pixels by default. Click the Advanced expand button (❯), then use the Pixel Aspect Ratio drop down menu to choose an aspect ratio other than square:

To specify a different Pixel Aspect Ratio for an existing image, choose Image>Pixel Aspect Ratio. Select an aspect ratio from the sub-menu.

You can also use the Fill command to fill selections with color.

When you need a fresh, completely blank canvas to work on, you can create a new file.

1   To create a new file, choose File>New. Enter a name for the new document (or leave this as Untitled and do a Save As later).

2   Specify Width and Height settings, or choose dimensions from the Preset menu. If you have copied pixels to the clipboard, the Preset menu is automatically set to Clipboard and the Width and Height entry boxes automatically reflect the dimensions of the elements on the clipboard.

3   Enter a resolution and choose a color mode. You can also specify whether you want to create a file with 8-bits per channel, or 16-bits per channel.

4   Select one of the Background Contents options to specify the canvas background you want to begin with, then OK the dialog box.

5   To change the color of the canvas after you click OK in the New dialog box, select a foreground color (see Chapter Four, "Image and Color Basics"). Next, choose Edit>Fill. Choose Foreground Color from the Use pop-up. Make sure Opacity is set to 100% and Mode is Normal. Click OK.

Photomerge

The Photomerge command allows you to combine two or more images to create a panorama.

1 Open the images you want to use for the photomerge composition. Choose File>Automate>Photomerge.

2 In the Photomerge dialog box make sure the Use drop down menu is set to Open Files – these are the files already open in Photoshop. Leave the Attempt to Automatically Arrange Source Images option selected to allow Photoshop to attempt to match and blend the source images automatically. Deselect this option if you want to arrange the individual source images yourself. If Photoshop is unable to arrange the images automatically a warning dialog box appears. OK the warning and arrange the images manually.

Use standard Photoshop techniques to zoom in and out on the image and to move around in the work area. You can also use the Navigator view box in the same way as you use the Navigator palette in the Photoshop window:

The lightbox area allows you to store source images not currently in use in the photomerge composition.

You can drag source image thumbnails out of the lightbox area to become part of the photomerge composition and you can also drag images out of the work area back into the lightbox to remove them from the photomerge composition.

3   To manually create the photomerge composition, drag the source image thumbnails that appear in the lightbox area at the top of the Photomerge window into the main composition work area. Use the Select Image tool ( ) to reposition the images.

4   If necessary, with the Select Image tool selected, position your cursor on an image in the work area, then drag to reposition each image manually. Use the Rotate Image ( ) tool to rotate images in the work area.

5   Make sure you leave the Snap to Image option selected to allow Photoshop to analyze the images and automatically locate and position areas of common pixel values. Select the Keep as Layers option to save the individual source images on separate layers. This can be useful if you need to color correct individual source images at a later stage.

6   To reduce the effect of color differences in the original source images select the Advanced Blending option. This option blends variations in color and tones in areas of detail over small restricted areas, whilst broad colors and tones are blended over larger areas.

7   To open the photomerge composition in the main Photoshop window click the OK button. To save the composition without opening it in Photoshop click the Save Composition as button.

Image and Color Basics

There are a number of common techniques and tasks, such as cropping an image and making it larger or smaller, or changing the resolution to suit your final output needs, that you need to undertake on many of the images on which you work. This chapter covers a range of these tasks.

Defining colors is another essential aspect of using Photoshop and there is a range of techniques that can be used. The color controls in the Toolbox indicate the current foreground and background colors.

Covers

Chapter Four

Rotating an Image

You can quickly rotate an image if you have scanned it at the wrong orientation, or, for example, if you have imported an image in landscape orientation from a digital camera.

When using arbitrary rotation, position a ruler guide (see page 23, "Ruler Guides and Grids") to help determine how far you need to rotate:

To rotate an image in set increments, use Image>Rotate Canvas. Choose one of the preset increments. CW stands for clockwise, CCW for counter-clockwise. In the example above, you would choose 90 degrees counter-clockwise to rotate the Beijing Duck seller upright.

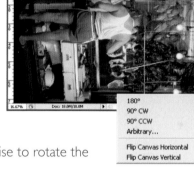

Sometimes you need to adjust an image a few degrees to make up for a poor original photograph or slightly misaligned scan:

To rotate in precise amounts, choose Image>Rotate Canvas>Arbitrary. Enter a value for the angle. Choose the clockwise (CW) or counter-clockwise (CCW) radio button, then OK the dialog box.

Choose Image>Rotate Canvas>Flip Canvas Horizontal/ Vertical to flip the entire image across its vertical or horizontal axis.

You may need to recrop the image. Use the Smart Sharpen or Unsharp Mask filters to compensate for any blurring due to the rotation.

Resizing without Resampling

When you resize an image without resampling, you make the image larger or smaller without changing the total number of pixels in the image. The overall dimensions of the image change, the file size remains the same, but the resolution of the image goes up if you make the image smaller, down if you make the image larger.

Smaller without resampling

Original

Larger without resampling

To decrease the size of your image without resampling, choose Image>Image Size. Make sure that Resample Image is deselected. Enter a lower value in the Width or Height entry boxes,

or enter a higher resolution. The other measurements update automatically. The file size of the image remains the same – no pixels were added. The resolution has increased – the same number of pixels are packed into a smaller area.

2 To increase the size of your image without resampling, enter a higher value in the Width or Height entry box, or enter a lower resolution. The file size of the image remains the same, but the resolution has decreased.

Resampling Up

Resampling up involves interpolation. Interpolation is used when Photoshop has to add information – new pixels – that didn't previously exist in an image. Choose an interpolation option from the pop-up in the Image Size dialog box. Bicubic gives best results, but takes longest. Nearest Neighbor is quickest, but least accurate. Bilinear gives a medium quality result. Bicubic Smoother is based on Bicubic, it is intended for enlarging images and can produce smoother results. Bicubic Sharper can be useful for reducing the size of images, when preparing them for the Web.

Bicubic	∨
Nearest Neighbor	
Bilinear	
Bicubic	
Bicubic Smoother	
Bicubic Sharper	

As far as possible, try to avoid resampling up. You are adding pixels to the image, without increasing the quality and detail in the image. You get better results if you scan the image at the size at which you intend to use it and at the resolution required for output.

When you resample up, new pixels are added to the image, so the file size increases. Resampling takes place when you increase the resolution setting, or the width/height settings with the Resample Image option selected. This example starts with a 2in by 2in image at 150 ppi.

1 Choose Image>Image Size. To keep the overall dimensions of the image, but increase the resolution, make sure that Resample Image is selected. Select Constrain Proportions so that the image's original proportions are maintained. Enter a higher value in the Resolution box.

Image Size

Pixel Dimensions: 263.7K

Width: 300 pixels
Height: 300 pixels

Document Size:

Width: 2 inches
Height: 2 inches
Resolution: 150 pixels/inch

☑ Scale Styles
☑ Constrain Proportions
☑ Resample Image: Bicubic

OK
Cancel
Auto...

When you are working in the Image Size dialog box, to reset the dialog box values to their initial settings, hold down Alt/option on the keyboard. The Cancel button becomes a Reset button. Click the Reset button.

You can use this technique in other Photoshop dialog boxes as well.

2 The file size and total number of pixels increase, but the Width and Height settings remain the same.

Image Size

Pixel Dimensions: 1.03M (was 263.7K)

Width: 600 pixels
Height: 600 pixels

Document Size:

Width: 2 inches
Height: 2 inches
Resolution: 300 pixels/inch

☑ Scale Styles
☑ Constrain Proportions
☑ Resample Image: Bicubic

You now have an image which is the same overall size, but which has more pixels in the same area, and therefore its resolution is increased:

When you resample an image, blurring may occur due to the process of interpolation. You can use the Smart Sharpen or Unsharp Mask filters to partially compensate for this. (See pages 173–175.)

3 To make the overall dimensions of the image bigger, but to keep the same resolution, again make sure that Resample Image is selected. Select Constrain Proportions to keep width and height proportional. Enter a higher value in either the Width or Height entry boxes. (The other entry boxes update automatically if you select Constrain Proportions.)

Image Size

Pixel Dimensions: 1.03M (was 263.7K)
Width: 600 pixels
Height: 600 pixels

Document Size:
Width: 4 inches
Height: 4 inches
Resolution: 150 pixels/inch

☑ Scale Styles
☑ Constrain Proportions
☑ Resample Image: Bicubic

OK
Cancel
Auto...

4 The overall dimensions of the image have now increased. The file size and total number of pixels have also increased, but the resolution remains the same.

Sampling Down

You sometimes need to resample down to maintain an optimal balance between the resolution needed for acceptable final output and file size considerations. There is little point in working with an image at too high a resolution if some of the image information is redundant at final output.

Resampling down means discarding pixels. The result is a smaller file size. Resampling down occurs when you decrease the resolution setting, or the width/height settings with the Resample Image option selected.

Choose View>Print Size to get a representation on screen of the physical size of the image when printed.

These examples start with a 2 by 2 inch image at 300 ppi.

Choose Image>Image Size. To keep the overall dimensions of the image, but decrease the resolution, make sure that Resample Image is selected. Leave Constrain Proportions selected, so that the image's original proportions are maintained. Reduce the value in the Resolution box.

Image Size

Pixel Dimensions: 1.03M

Width: 600 pixels
Height: 600 pixels

OK
Cancel
Auto...

Document Size:

Width: 2 inches
Height: 2 inches
Resolution: 300 pixels/inch

☑ Scale Styles
☑ Constrain Proportions
☑ Resample Image: Bicubic

2 The file size goes down and the total number of pixels decreases, whilst the Width and Height settings remain the same.

Image Size

Pixel Dimensions: 263.7K (was 1.03M)

Width: 300 pixels
Height: 300 pixels

Document Size:

Width: 2 inches
Height: 2 inches
Resolution: 150 pixels/inch

☑ Scale Styles
☑ Constrain Proportions
☑ Resample Image: Bicubic Smoother

You now have an image which is the same overall size, but with fewer pixels in the same area, and therefore its resolution is lower:

3   To reduce the overall dimensions of the image, but keep the image at the same resolution, make sure that Resample Image is selected. (Select Constrain Proportions to keep the width and height proportional.) Enter a lower value in either the Width or Height entry box. (The other entry box updates automatically if you select Constrain Proportions.)

4   The overall dimensions of the image have now decreased. The file size and the total number of pixels have also decreased, but the resolution remains the same.

Cropping an Image

Use the Crop tool to crop unwanted areas of an image and reduce the file size.

Press C on the keyboard to select the Crop tool, then press Return/Enter to show the Crop tool Options bar if it is not already showing.

1 Select the Crop tool. Position your cursor on the image, then click and drag to define the crop area. Don't worry if you don't get the crop exactly right first time. The area of the image outside the crop dims to indicate the parts of the image to be discarded.

With a crop marquee active, use the Shield Cropped Area option in the Options bar to hide/show the crop shading overlay. You can also change the color and/or opacity of the crop shading:

2 To reposition the crop marquee, place your cursor inside the marquee, then click and drag. To resize the crop marquee, place your cursor on one of the 8 handles around the marquee (the cursor changes to a bi-directional arrow), then click and drag. To rotate the marquee, position your cursor just outside the marquee (the cursor changes shape to indicate rotation), then click and drag in a circular direction.

Hold down Shift, then click and drag on a corner handle to resize the crop marquee in proportion.

The Crop tool snaps to the edge of the image. To prevent the snap effect, hold down Ctrl/Command+Shift as you resize the crop marquee.

3 When you are satisfied with the position and size of the crop marquee, click the Commit button in the Options bar, or press Return/Enter to crop the image. Alternatively, you can double-click inside the crop marquee. The areas outside the marquee are discarded. Click the Cancel button, or press the Esc key if you want to remove the crop marquee without cropping.

Adding a Border

Borders are useful when you need additional space around the edges of your image.

1 Choose Image>Canvas Size. Use the measurement pop-up menus to choose a unit of measurement. Enter increased values for the Width and/or Height fields.

2 To specify where the border is added relative to the image, click one of the placement squares. This sets the relative position of the image and the border. The white square represents the position of the image, the other squares the position of the border.

3 Choose a color from the Canvas extension color pop-up menu to specify the color of the border. OK the dialog to add the border. This increases the file size as the command adds pixels to the image.

Image Modes

Image modes are fundamental to working in Photoshop. When you open an image the mode is indicated in the title bar of the image window. There are eight different modes in Photoshop. Use modes as appropriate to your working requirements. Then, depending on output or printing requirements, if necessary, convert to a different mode.

RGB mode

Images are typically scanned or captured in RGB mode. When you start work with a color image it is usually best to work in RGB mode, as this is faster than CMYK mode and allows you to use all of Photoshop's commands and features, providing greatest flexibility.

The disadvantage of working in RGB mode, if your image will be printed commercially, is that RGB allows a greater gamut of colors than you can print. At some stage, some of the brightest, most vibrant colors may lose their brilliance when the image is brought within the CMYK gamut.

CMYK mode

To retain the flexibility of working in RGB mode, but see an on-screen CMYK preview of your image, first make sure that View>Proof Setup is set to Working CMYK, then choose View>Proof Colors. (You may have to wait a few seconds when you choose this option as Photoshop builds its color conversion tables.) The title bar of the image changes to indicate that you are working with an RGB image, but previewing in CMYK:

Nons1.tif @ 100% (RGB/8/CMYK)

Convert to CMYK when the image is to be printed commercially and you have finished making changes.

To place a color image in a page layout application from where it will be color separated, you need to convert from RGB to CMYK. When you convert from RGB to CMYK, Photoshop adjusts any colors in the RGB image that fall outside the CMYK gamut to their nearest printable color. (See Page 63, for details on gamut warnings.)

You can also select View>Gamut Warning (Ctrl/Command+ Shift+Y), to highlight (in gray) areas of the image that are out of gamut.

Indexed Color mode

This mode reduces your image to 256 colors or less and is frequently used for multimedia and Web images.

Duotone

For details on using Duotone mode see page 60.

You must first convert to Grayscale mode before you can convert to Duotone mode.

Grayscale mode

When you are not printing an image in color you can convert to Grayscale mode to make working faster and file size smaller.

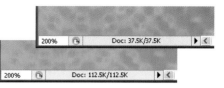

Lab mode

This mode uses the CIE Lab model which has one channel for luminosity, an "a" channel representing colors blue to yellow and a "b" channel for magenta to green. A significant advantage to this mode is that its gamut encompasses that of both CMYK and RGB modes.

Bitmap mode

This mode reduces everything to black or white pixels. The image becomes a 1-bit image.

Multichannel mode

Multichannel mode uses 256 levels of gray in each channel. When you convert RGB or CMYK images to multichannel mode, the original channels in the image are converted to spot color channels. Multichannel mode is an advanced option – only use it if you have a detailed understanding of the printing process.

To convert from one mode to another, choose Image>Mode and choose the mode you want from the sub-menu. Depending on which mode you are converting from and to, you may get a message box warning you of any consequences of converting to the new mode and asking you to confirm your request.

Bitmap
Grayscale
Duotone
Indexed Color...
✔ RGB Color
CMYK Color
Lab Color
Multichannel

✔ 8 Bits/Channel
16 Bits/Channel
32 Bits/Channel

Color Table...

Adobe Photoshop

⚠ Discard color information?

[OK] [Cancel]

☐ Don't show again

Duotone Mode

Duotone is a very popular effect used to give added tonal depth to a grayscale image by printing with black and another color.

You can only access Duotone mode when you have converted to Grayscale mode.

To create a duotone, choose Image>Mode>Duotone. Choose from the Type pop-up whether you want to create a duotone (two inks), a tritone (three inks) or a quadtone (four inks).

When you start working with Photoshop, click on the Load button and try using one of the preset duotone settings that can be found in: Program Files>Adobe>Adobe Photoshop CS2>Presets>Duotones:

To choose a second color for the duotone, click the "Ink 2" color box (below the black ink box). This takes you into the Color Libraries dialog box. Choose a color. Click the Picker button if you want to use the Color Picker. OK the dialog box.

Make sure you save duotones in EPS or PDF format so that they color-separate correctly from page layout applications.

To specify the ink coverage for both colors, click first on the Ink 1 Curve box, then the Ink 2 box. In the Duotone Curve dialog box, drag the curve to the desired position, or enter values in the % entry boxes to adjust the ink coverage curve. Click Preview in the Duotone Options dialog to preview the result in the image window before you OK the dialog boxes.

Foreground & Background Colors

The foreground color is applied when you first create type, and when you use the Paint Bucket, Line, Pencil, and Brush tools.

The background color is the color you erase to when you use the Eraser tool, or when you delete or move a selection on the Background layer.

When you are working with foreground and background controls you can also switch colors, and you can quickly change back to the default colors, black and white.

You can change the background and foreground colors using the Eyedropper tool, the Color Picker palette, the Color palette and the Swatches palette.

Press X on the keyboard to switch background and foreground colors. Press D on the keyboard to revert to the default foreground and background colors.

1 To switch background to foreground and vice versa, click once on the Switch Colors arrow.

2 To revert to black and white as the default background and foreground colors, click the Default Colors icon.

Eyedropper & Color Sampler Tools

The Eyedropper tool

The Eyedropper tool provides a
quick and convenient way to pick up
foreground and background color from an area of the image you
are working on, or from another inactive Photoshop image window.

1. To set the foreground color, click on the Eyedropper tool. Position your cursor, then click once on the image. The Set foreground color box in the Toolbox now represents the color where you clicked.

2. To set the background color, hold down Alt/option then click on the image. The Set background color box in the Toolbox now indicates the color on which you clicked.

3. To set the Sample Size, use the Sample Size pop-up menu in the Options bar to choose a value. Point Sample reads the precise value of the pixel on which you click. 3 by 3 and 5 by 5 take average values of the pixels where you click.

To hide/show
the sample
points, choose
Hide/Show Color
Samplers from
the Info palette menu.

The Color Sampler tool

Use the Color Sampler tool (with the
Info palette) to set up to four sample
points which you can refer to as you make
adjustments to color values.
Each time you click in the
image window with the Color
Sampler tool, you set a sample
point. Each point creates an
extra pane in the Info palette.
To delete a sample point, drag
it out of the image window
with the Color Sampler tool.

The Color Picker Palette

Using the Color Picker palette is a powerful and flexible way of choosing foreground and background colors. You can use a number of different color models to create color.

Press the Tab key to move the highlight through the entry boxes in the dialog box.

To create a Process color using the Color Picker, click once on either the Set foreground or Set background color box. Enter values in the CMYK

entry boxes. A preview of the color appears in the Current Color swatch, above the Previous Color swatch.

A warning triangle – the Gamut alarm – appears next to the Current/Previous color boxes if you create a color that cannot be printed using CMYK inks. Click the warning triangle to choose the nearest printable color:

OK the dialog box. The color you defined now becomes the foreground or background color, depending on which box you clicked in Step 1.

You can also create colors using the Color Slider and the Color field. The next example uses Hue, Saturation and Brightness values. Use the same techniques for RGB and Lab color models.

The small box below the warning triangle indicates the nearest printable color.

To create a color using Hue, Saturation and Brightness (HSB) values, first click the Hue (H) radio button.

Click on the Color Slider bar, or drag the slider triangles on either side of the bar, to choose a hue or color. This sets one of the three HSB values. The number in the Hue entry box represents the hue you have chosen.

To create a Web-safe color, select the Only Web Colors option. Fewer colors are represented in the Color Field; each color exists in the Web palette which consists of 216 colors.

3 Next, click in the Color Field to set the other two variables – Saturation and Brightness. Clicking to the left of the field reduces the saturation, clicking to the right increases the saturation of the selected hue. Clicking near the bottom decreases brightness, clicking near the top increases brightness for the selected hue.

4 If you click on the Saturation button, the Color Slider now represents saturation (from 0–100) and the Color field allows you to choose Hue and Brightness values. When you click the Brightness radio button, the slider represents Brightness and the Color field represents Hue and Saturation.

Choosing Custom Colors

You can access a range of color-matching systems such as PANTONE, Toyo Color Finder and Focoltone Color System using the Color Libraries dialog box.

If the Web Colors Only option is deselected, the Non-Web Color alert appears if you create a color that is not in the Web palette. Click the Web alert icon to move the color to the nearest Web-safe color:

1 In the Color Picker dialog box, click the Color Libraries button. Use the Book pop-up menu to select a color matching system.

2 If you know the ink number of the color you want, you can enter the number on the keyboard. Alternatively, click in the color slider bar to the right of the ink color boxes. This moves you to a general range of colors. Use the scroll bars at the top and bottom of the sliders to find the specific color you want. Click on the color you want to select, then click OK.

In the Color Libraries dialog box, click the Picker button to return to the Color Picker dialog box.

The Color Palette

You can also use the Color palette (Window>Colors) to mix new colors.

Click the active color selection box to display the Color Picker palette.

1 First identify which color selection box is "active". There are two boxes, Set foreground color and Set background color. The active box is outlined in black.

2 Continue with step 3 if the correct box is active, or click the inactive box to make it the active box if necessary.

During step 3, if you create a color that is outside the CMYK color gamut, the gamut alert warning triangle appears. You can click on the alert triangle to set the color to the nearest CMYK equivalent. The nearest CMYK equivalent appears in a box next to the alert triangle:

3 Drag the Color slider triangles below the Color slider bars, or enter values in the entry boxes to the right of the palette. You can also click on a color in the Color Bar running along the bottom of the Color palette. The Color Bar contains every color in the CMYK spectrum as a default setting.

4 Use the palette menu triangle (⊙) in the top right of the palette to change the color model for the sliders.

5 Choose an option from the bottom half of the palette menu to specify the color model for the colors in the Color Bar at the bottom of the palette.

Dock to Palette Well

Grayscale Slider
✔ RGB Sliders
HSB Sliders
CMYK Sliders
Lab Sliders
Web Color Sliders

Copy Color as HTML

RGB Spectrum
✔ CMYK Spectrum
Grayscale Ramp
Current Colors

Make Ramp Web Safe

The Swatches Palette

You can use the Swatches palette (Window>Swatches) to set foreground and background colors, and you can also use it to create custom palettes which you can save and then reload into a different image.

See page 28 for details on loading and saving custom palette settings.

1 To select a foreground color from the Swatches palette, click on a color swatch. To select a background color, hold down Ctrl/Command and then click on a color swatch.

You can customize the Swatches palette by adding and deleting colors in the palette.

2 To add color to the swatches, select a foreground color. Position your cursor in an empty area of the Swatches palette. (The cursor changes to a paint bucket.) Then click. Enter a name for the new swatch, then click OK to add the current foreground color to the Swatches palette.

Position your cursor on a swatch in the Swatches palette, hold down Control (Mac), or click the right mouse button (PC), to access the context sensitive menu:

```
New Swatch...
Rename Swatch...
Delete Swatch
```

3 To delete a color swatch, hold down Alt/option (Mac) or Alt (Windows) and then click on a color swatch.

4 Use the Swatches palette menu to reset the Swatches palette to its default settings, or to choose a different color palette from the list.

The Painting Tools

The Brush and Pencil tools apply the foreground color to pixels in your image as you drag across them. By default, the Brush tool creates strokes with softened edges and the Pencil tool creates hard-edged lines. You can use the Brushes palette to determine the shape, size and type of brush stroke and to customize the brush shape and brush dynamics – the way the brush behaves as it colors pixels.

You can also save a customized brush as a "preset" brush. This allows you to create your own collection of custom brush effects that you can access quickly and easily whenever you need to.

Covers

Chapter Five

The Brush Preset Picker

The Brush Preset Picker allows quick, convenient access to a range of standard, preset brushes.

Rest your cursor on the brush thumbnail in the brush presets scroll box to see a descriptive help label for the tool:

1 To select a brush, click on the Brush tool to select it, then click the Brush pop-up triangle icon in the Options bar.

When you make changes to Mode, Opacity and Flow in the Options bar, these settings remain in force when you choose a different brush from the Brush Preset Picker palette.

2 Click on a brush you want to use in the scroll box. A representation of the shape of the brush appears in the left column of the scroll box, a thumbnail of the stroke appears to the right. The number beneath the brush icon indicates the diameter of the brush in pixels.

For circular shape brushes, use the Hardness slider to increase/decrease the hardness setting for the edge of the brush. (See page 74 for further information on setting Hardness).

3 To change the size of the brush, drag the Master Diameter slider to increase/decrease the size of the brush, or enter a value in pixels in the Size Entry box. Click the Use Sample Size button to return to the original size of the brush if you have made changes to the Master Diameter. (This option is only available for brush tip shapes created originally from a sample of pixels).

To constrain your painting strokes to straight lines, click with the Painting tool to position the start of the stroke, move your cursor (do not click and drag) then hold down Shift and click to end the stroke.

4 Create settings for Mode, Opacity and Flow in the Options bar and choose the Airbrush option if required.

5 Position your cursor in the image window, then press and drag to apply the foreground color using the current brush characteristics and the brush settings in the Options bar.

Remember to choose the foreground color you want to paint with before you start to use a painting tool.

To change the Opacity setting using the keyboard, type numbers on the keyboard. For example, type 7 to specify an Opacity setting of 70%. Type 7 then 8 in quick succession to create a setting of 78%.

For a description of blending modes, see pages 79–81.

The Airbrush option is selected when the icon in the Options bar has a border around it:

Opacity

Opacity (Brush, Pencil, History Brush, Art History Brush, Gradient, Paint Bucket, Clone Stamp and Pattern Stamp tools) controls how completely pixels are covered with the foreground color when you drag across them.

Make sure the Opacity slider is at 100% if you want to completely cover the pixels you drag across. (Soft-edged brushes only partially cover pixels around the edge of the painting stroke to create the soft edge effect.) Reducing the Opacity setting gives less complete results in the area you drag across, creating a semi-transparent, partially-covered effect.

Flow

Flow controls how quickly paint is applied when you drag the brush across the image.

Airbrush

Select the Airbrush option to imitate the effect of spraying paint with an airbrush. The Airbrush option works best with soft-edged brushes and reduced Opacity and Flow settings.

The Brushes Palette

The Brushes palette provides access to a wide variety of options for controlling the appearance and characteristics of your brush strokes. You can use preset brushes, or you can create your own custom brushes using a variety of interchangeable settings.

If the Brushes palette appears dimmed, you do not have an appropriate Painting or Editing tool selected.

1 To create custom brush characteristics, select a painting tool. By default, the Brushes palette is docked in the Palette Well (on the right-hand side of the Options bar). Click on the Brushes tab to display the Brushes palette.

2 Make sure the Brush Presets option is selected. Click on a preset brush in the scroll list. You can rest your cursor on a preset brush in the scroll list to show a help label which indicates the settings currently applied to the brush. Depending on the brush preset you click on, the various customized settings already applied to the brush, visible in the left hand column, change accordingly.

Drag the Brushes tab from the Palette Well if you prefer the palette to behave as a standard floating palette.

You can also use the Brushes palette for setting the brush characteristics for Editing tools.

3 To customize the preset brush by adding your own brush settings, click the checkboxes to the left of the brush characteristic labels. The preview pane at the bottom of the palette updates to indicate the effect on the brush. (In this example the 13-pixel, soft-edged brush is selected, with Scattering, Shape Dynamics, Smoothing and Wet Edges also applied.)

4 Drag the Master Diameter slider to change the size of the brush, or enter a value in pixels in the Size Entry box.

Selecting the Airbrush option in the Options palette is the equivalent of selecting Airbrush from the effects list in the Brushes palette.

5 Click on the Brush Tip Shape button to change shape settings such as Angle, Roundness, Hardness and Spacing if required. (See page 74 for further information.)

6 Click the brush characteristic label (to the right of the check box) to access a range of controls for the option. (See page 72 for information on creating custom brush characteristic settings).

Use the Brush Presets Picker palette when you want to quickly select a brush from the existing set of brushes. Use the Brushes palette to select a preset brush and also to create and design your own custom brushes.

7 Create settings for Mode, Opacity and Flow in the Options bar.

8 If you click on a different brush in the scroll list, any custom settings for the previously selected brush are lost. Create a tool preset if you want to save the settings on a more permanent basis. (See page 76 for further information).

9 Position your cursor in the image window, then click and drag to create the required paint stroke.

Custom Brush Settings

Preset brushes can be customized using the style options on the left side of the Brushes palette together with the settings which control the Brush Tip Shape. Effects above the gray divider bar have controls that allow you to customize each effect. Style options below the gray divider bar cannot be edited.

1   To create custom settings for a brush effect such as Shape Dynamics, click the effect label (the words Shape Dynamics) – not the checkbox. The controls available for each brush effect appear on the right of the dialog box.

To understand what Photoshop refers to as paint marks, select a simple preset brush, click the Brush Tip Shape button, then drag the spacing slider to the right. This indicates visually how the individual paint marks form a paint stroke when you drag the Brush tool in the image window.

2   Experiment with the settings available. The preview box at the bottom of the palette updates to reflect changes you make to the settings.

Shape Dynamics
The Shape Dynamics options control the manner in which brush marks in the painting stroke change as you drag your cursor in the image window.

Scattering
Scattering settings allow you to specify how the position of the paint marks in a stroke is varied and also control the number of paint marks in a stroke.

Texture
Use texture settings on a brush to associate the brush with a pattern to create paint strokes that appear to be painted on a textured canvas.

Dual Brush
Dual Brush uses two tips to create the brush stroke. Set options for the primary tip using options in the Brush Tip Shape area. Set options for the secondary tip in the Dual Brush area.

Color Dynamics
Color Dynamics settings control how the color of the painting stroke changes over the length of the stroke.

Other Dynamics
Other Dynamics control the speed with which paint is applied and the opacity of the paint in the stroke.

Noise
Noise has the most apparent effect around the edges of soft-edged brushes and creates a random scattering of pixels.

Wet Edges
Wet Edges creates a stroke that is darker around the edges and translucent inside the stroke, imitating the uneven build up of paint in a watercolor.

Airbrush
The Airbrush option on a soft-edged brush with a medium to low Opacity setting simulates the effect of spraying paint with an airbrush.

Smoothing
Smoothing helps create smoother curves in brush strokes.

Protect Texture
Select the Protect Texture option to keep texture effects consistent when painting with different textured brush tips. The option applies the same pattern and scale to all preset brushes with a texture.

Brush Tip Shape Settings

The Brush Tip Shape options area of the Brushes palette provides a further set of controls for specifying the appearance of a brush stroke.

To create custom brush tip shape settings for a brush, first select a brush from the Brush Presets list. Then click the Brush Tip Shape button in the Brushes palette. Enter values for Diameter, Hardness, Spacing, Angle and Roundness in the brush tip settings area.

To save custom brush tip settings for future use, see page 76 – "Creating Brush Preset Tools".

Diameter
Enter a value in pixels for the diameter of your brush from 1–2500. Brush sizes too large to be represented at their actual size will display with the diameter indicated as a number.

Hardness
A setting of 100% gives a hard-edged brush. Lower settings produce soft-edged brushes. The lower you take this setting, the more diffuse the resultant stroke when you paint with the brush. Even with settings of 100%, the edge of the brush-stroke is anti-aliased.

Spacing
Spacing is measured as a percentage of brush size. 25% is the default setting for standard brushes. Higher settings begin to create non-continuous strokes.

Select the Flip X or Flip Y checkbox to flip the paint mark across its vertical or horizontal axis to change the direction of the brush effect.

Angle and Roundness
Use these controls together to create a stroke which thickens and thins like a calligraphic pen. You can enter values in the entry boxes, or drag the arrow indicator to change the angle, and drag the diameter dots to change the diameter.

The Pencil Tool

You can use the Pencil tool to draw freeform lines. The lines you draw with the Pencil tool are always hard-edged – in other words, the edges of your lines are not anti-aliased. The Pencil tool paints or draws with the foreground color.

1 To draw a line, first select the Pencil tool. Set a brush size using the Brush Preset Picker. (See page 68). Or use the Brushes palette to create custom brush settings for the tool. (See page 72).

2 Use the Pencil Options bar to specify: Blending Mode, Opacity and Auto Erase options.

3 Click and drag to create a freeform pencil stroke. Hold down Shift, then drag to constrain the pencil stroke vertically or horizontally.

4 To create a straight pencil stroke between two points, click, move the cursor to a new position (do not click and drag), hold down Shift, then click again.

Auto Erase
Select this checkbox to use the Pencil tool to paint out or erase areas of foreground color using the current background color.

Creating Brush Preset Tools

Create a Brush tool preset when you have created custom brush settings that you want to be able to reuse, without having to first recreate the custom settings.

1   To create a Brush tool preset, select the Brush tool, then use the Brushes palette to create custom settings for the brush.

2   Choose Window> Tool Presets, to show the Tool Presets palette if it is not already showing.

3   Choose New Tool Preset from the palette menu. Enter a name for the tool preset in the New Tool Preset dialog box.

A tool preset allows you to save custom brush settings so that you can access them quickly and easily, whenever you need to, without having to first recreate the settings.

4   To access the new tool preset, make sure you have the Brush tool selected, then click the Brush tool presets triangle in the Options bar. Click on the tool preset in the drop-down list.

The Gradient Tool

You can use the Gradient tool to create transitions from one color to another. You can also create multicolored gradients. There are options for Linear, Radial, Angle, Reflected and Diamond gradients. You can apply a gradient fill to a selection, or to an entire active layer.

To create a gradient fill, select the Gradient tool. Choose a gradient type from the Options bar.

Hold down Shift as you click and drag to constrain a linear gradient to 45° increments.

Select a Blending mode and set Opacity. Use the Gradient pop-up to choose one of the preset gradients.

Position your cursor where you want the gradient to start, then click and drag. The angle and distance you drag the cursor defines the angle and distance of a linear gradient, or the radius of a radial gradient. (Click and drag from the center out to create Radial, Angle, Reflected and Diamond gradient fills.)

For a linear gradient, the start and end colors fill any part of the selection that you do not drag the cursor across. For radial gradients, the end color fills the remaining area.

For basic gradient fills you can leave the Transparency and Dither options selected. Choose the Reverse option to reverse the order of the colors in the gradient.

Linear   Radial   Angle   Reflected   Diamond

The Paint Bucket Tool

You can use the Paint Bucket tool to color pixels with the foreground color, based on a tolerance setting. It works in a similar way to the Magic Wand tool, but in this case filling adjoining pixels that fall within the tolerance setting. You can use the Paint Bucket tool within a selection or on the entire image.

1   To fill an area with the foreground color, select the Paint Bucket tool. Leave the Fill pop-up set to Foreground. Enter a value from 0–255 in the Tolerance box. The higher you set the value, the greater the pixel range the Paint Bucket fills.

The Anti-aliased option creates a slightly soft edge in the areas that the Paint Bucket fills.

2   Set Opacity, Blending mode, Anti-aliased and All Layers options as required. Position your cursor then click on the image.

3   You can use the Paint Bucket to fill with a pattern previously saved into the pattern library. Use the Fill pop-up to choose Pattern, then use the Pattern pop-up palette to choose an available pattern.

You cannot use the Paint Bucket on images in Bitmap mode.

4   Deselect the Contiguous option to allow the Paint Bucket to color pixels anywhere in the image, provided that they fall within the Tolerance setting.

Blending Modes

Normal ▾

Normal
Dissolve
Behind
Clear

Darken
Multiply
Color Burn
Linear Burn

Lighten
Screen
Color Dodge
Linear Dodge

Overlay
Soft Light
Hard Light
Vivid Light
Linear Light
Pin Light
Hard Mix

Difference
Exclusion

Hue
Saturation
Color
Luminosity

Choose blending modes from the pop-up menu in the Painting Tool Options palette. The various paint modes in combination with opacity/pressure settings have a selective control on which pixels are affected when you use the painting and editing tools. The result is more of a blending of the paint color and the color of the base pixels than simply one color replacing another.

Dissolve

Produces a grainy, chalk-like effect. Not all pixels are colored as you drag across the image, leaving gaps and holes in the stroke. Reduce the Opacity setting to control the effect.

Clear

Makes pixels transparent. You can only access this mode on a layer with the Lock Transparency option deselected. Available for the Brush, Paint Bucket, Pencil and Line tools.

Behind

Only available when you are working on a layer with a transparent background. Make sure Lock Transparency is deselected for the layer. Use Behind to paint behind the existing pixels on a layer. Paint appears in the transparent areas, but does not affect the existing pixels.

The blending modes allow you to make changes to an image using the painting and editing tools in a more selective and subtle way than simply painting with the foreground color. The color you paint with (the blend color) combines with the color of the pixels you drag across (the base color) to produce a different color depending on the blending mode you select.

Darken

Applies the paint color to pixels that are lighter than the paint color – doesn't change pixels darker than the paint color.

Multiply

Combines the color you are painting with the color of the pixels you drag across, to produce a color that is darker than the original colors.

Color Burn

Darkens the base color by increasing the contrast in base color pixels, depending on the blend color. More pronounced when paint color is dark. Blending with white has no effect.

Refer to the original image below for comparison purposes. This image uses Normal blending mode:

Blending modes are also available in the Layers palette and in the Fill Path, Fill, Stroke and Fade dialog boxes.

For circular shape brushes, use the Hardness slider to increase/decrease the hardness setting for the edge of the brush. (See page 74 for further information on setting Hardness.)

Linear Burn
Darkens the base color by decreasing brightness depending on the blend color used. Blending with white has no effect.

Lighten
Replaces pixels darker than the paint color, but does not change pixels lighter than the paint color.

Screen
Produces the opposite effect to Multiply. It multiplies the opposite of the original color by the painting color and has the effect of lightening the pixels.

Color Dodge
Brightens the base color by decreasing contrast. More pronounced when the paint color is light. Blending with black has no effect.

Linear Dodge
Brightens the base color by increasing the brightness depending on the blend color. Blending with black has no effect.

Overlay
This increases the contrast and saturation, combining the foreground color with the pixels you drag across. Highlights and shadows in the base color are preserved.

Soft Light
Creates a soft lighting effect. Lightens colors if the painting color is lighter than 50% gray, darkens colors if the painting color is darker than 50% gray.

Hard Light
Multiplies (darkens) or screens (lightens) pixels, depending on the paint color, and tends to increase contrast.

...cont'd

Vivid Light
Burns or Dodges base pixel colors by increasing or decreasing contrast depending on the blend color.

Linear Light
Burns or Dodges base pixel colors by increasing or decreasing brightness depending on the blend color.

Pin Light
Replaces base color pixels depending on whether the blend color is lighter or darker than 50% gray.

Difference
It looks at the brightness of pixels and the paint color, then subtracts paint brightness from pixel brightness. Depending on the result, it inverts the pixels.

Exclusion
The result is similar to Difference, but with lower contrast.

To constrain your painting strokes to straight lines, click with the Painting tool to position the start of the stroke, move your cursor (do not click and drag) then hold down Shift and click to end the stroke.

Hue
In color images, applies the hue (color) of the paint, without affecting the saturation or luminosity of the base pixels.

Saturation
Changes the saturation of pixels based on the saturation of the blend color, but does not affect hue or luminosity.

Luminosity
Changes the relative lightness/darkness of the pixels without affecting their hue/saturation.

Color
Applies the hue and saturation of the blend color; does not affect base pixel luminosity.

Creating Rasterized Shapes

A rasterized shape is a shape comprised of pixels. It is not based on a vector path and cannot be edited in the same way as a shape layer.

You cannot create a rasterized shape on a vector based shape layer or a type layer.

1   To create a rasterized shape, select a layer, or create a new layer. Select a foreground color for the shape.

2   Select either the Rectangle, Rounded Rectangle, Ellipse, Line, Polygon or Custom Shape tool.

■ Rectangle Tool	U
Rounded Rectangle Tool	U
Ellipse Tool	U
Polygon Tool	U
Line Tool	U
Custom Shape Tool	U

3   Select the Fill Pixels button in the Options bar.

The Polygon tool and the Custom Shape tools are not available in ImageReady.

4   Position your cursor in the image window. Drag diagonally to define the size of the shape. The shape appears in the window. It does not automatically create a new layer. A rasterized shape is the equivalent of creating a selection, then filling it with a color.

To create a custom shape, select the Custom Shape tool, then click on the Shape pop-up triangle to access the default shape library. Click on a shape to select it, then click and drag in the image window to define the size of the shape:

5   For the Polygon tool, you can set a number of sides for the shape in the Options bar. Click on the settings pop-up triangle to access further controls for creating polygons or stars.

Polygon Options

Radius:

☐ Smooth Corners

☐ Star

Indent Sides By:

☐ Smooth Indents

The Editing Tools

The editing tools – Blur and Sharpen, Smudge, Clone and Pattern Stamp, Dodge, Burn, Sponge, Eraser, Healing Brush, Patch and Color Replacement – let you edit or change pixels in a variety of ways.

The editing tools can be used within a selection or anywhere on an image. Use the Brush Preset Picker palette to specify a brush size for the editing tool. Many of the techniques and keyboard shortcuts covered for the painting tools apply to the editing tools as well.

Covers

Chapter Six

The Blur, Sharpen & Smudge Tools

The Blur and Sharpen Tools

Remember to set an appropriate brush size before you start working with the Blur/Sharpen tool.

The Blur and Sharpen tools are the two "focus" tools. The Blur tool works by reducing contrast between pixels and can be useful for disguising unwanted, jagged edges and softening edges between shapes. The Sharpen tool works by increasing the contrast between pixels.

You cannot use the Blur or Sharpen tools on an image in Bitmap or Indexed Color mode.

To blur or sharpen areas of your image, select the appropriate tool. In the Options bar, set the Blend mode, Strength and Use All Layers options, position your cursor on the image, then click and drag to blur or sharpen the pixels. Release the mouse then drag across the pixels again to intensify the effect. You may produce a coarse, grainy effect if you overuse the Sharpen tool. Use a low Strength setting and build up the effect gradually.

The Smudge Tool

Use the Smudge tool to create an effect similar to dragging your finger through wet paint. The Smudge tool picks up color from where you start to drag and smears it into adjacent colors.

Each Focus tool retains its own settings when you switch to one of the other tools in the group.

Select the Smudge tool. Set the Strength, position your cursor on the image, then start to drag across your image to smudge the colors. The higher the Strength setting, the more pronounced the effect.

Depending on whether the option is selected or deselected in the Options bar, hold down Alt/option to temporarily turn Finger Painting on or off.

2 Select the Finger Painting option if you want to begin the smudge with the current foreground color. Select the Use All Layers option to smudge colors from other layers in the image onto the layer you are working on. Leave this option deselected if you want the smudge to pick up color from pixels on the active or target layer only.

The Clone Stamp Tool

You can use the Clone Stamp tool to retouch an image by cloning or duplicating areas of it. This is very useful when you want to remove blemishes and scratches.

> **1** To clone an area of your image, select the Clone Stamp tool. Set an appropriate brush size using the Brush Preset Picker palette in the Options bar. Make sure that the Aligned option is selected.

| ▼ | Brush: 20 ▼ | Mode: Normal ▼ | Opacity: 100% ▶ | Flow: 100% ▶ | ✎ | ☑ Aligned |

Use the "[" or "]" keys on the keyboard to decrease/increase the size of editing tool brushes as you work.

2 Hold down Alt/option and click on the part of the image you want to clone.

3 Release Alt/option. Move the cursor to a different image part then click and drag. The pixels in the image where you drag are replaced by pixels cloned from the spot where you first clicked. A crosshair at the point where you first clicked indicates the pixels that are being cloned – the source point.

Clone – Aligned

With Aligned selected, the distance from the source point (shown by the crosshair) to the Clone Stamp cursor remains fixed. When you release the mouse, move the cursor, then continue to use the Clone Stamp tool, the relative position of the source point and the Rubber Stamp cursor remains constant, but you will now clone pixels from a different part of the image.

Clone – Non-aligned

With the Aligned option off, the source point – where you first click – remains the same. If you stop dragging with the Clone Stamp cursor, move to a different part of the image, then start dragging again, the pixels you clone continue to come from the original source point.

The Dodge, Burn and Sponge Tools

You cannot use the Dodge, Burn or Saturate/ Desaturate tools on an image in Bitmap or Indexed Color mode.

The Dodge, Burn, Saturate/Desaturate group of tools are sometimes referred to as the "toning" tools. The Dodge and Burn tools are based on the traditional photographic technique of decreasing the amount of exposure given to a specific area on a print to lighten it (dodging), or increasing the exposure to darken areas (burning-in).

The Dodge and Burn Tools

Use the Dodge tool to lighten pixels in your image; the Burn tool to darken pixels in your image.

It's a good idea to use a low exposure setting when you lighten areas of an image so that you build up the effect gradually.

1. To lighten or darken areas of an image, select the appropriate tool. Remember to choose an suitable brush size. A soft-edged brush usually creates the smoothest result.

2. In the Options bar, set the Range pop-up menu to Midtones, Shadows or Highlights to limit changes to the middle range of grays, the dark or light areas of the image respectively, and also set Exposure to control the intensity of the tool.

Each Toning tool retains its own settings when you switch to another tool in the same group.

3. Position your cursor on the image, then click and drag to lighten/ darken the pixels. Release the mouse then drag across the pixels again to intensify the effect.

The Sponge Tool

You can use the Sponge tool when you want to subtly increase or decrease color saturation in areas of your image.

In Grayscale mode, the Sponge tool has the effect of increasing or decreasing contrast.

To saturate/desaturate areas of an image, select the Sponge tool. Remember to select an appropriate brush size. Set the Mode pop-up to Saturate or Desaturate. Position your cursor on the image, then click and drag to alter the saturation.

The Eraser Tool

Eraser Tool   E

Use the Master Diameter setting in the Brush Preset Picker palette to specify the Eraser size when using the tool in Brush and Pencil mode.

Use the Eraser tool to erase portions of your image. The Eraser rubs out to the background color when you are working on the Background layer. It erases to transparency when you are working on any other layer, provided that the Transparency Lock option is not selected in the Layers palette.

1   To erase areas of your image, select the Eraser tool (E) to show Eraser options in the Options bar. Use the bar to specify brush size, Mode, Opacity, Flow, Airbrush and Erase to History options.

2   Click and drag on your image to erase to the background color or transparency, depending on the layer on which you are working.

Opacity
Use the Opacity setting to create the effect of partially erasing pixels in the image.

Mode
Use the Mode pop-up to choose an erase mode. The default is Brush. Block is useful when you need to erase along straight edges. The Block eraser is a fixed-size square.

Erase to History

Hold down Alt/option with the Eraser tool selected to access the Erase to History option temporarily. Click and drag across modified areas of the image to restore them to the specified state in the History palette.

Use the Erase to History option to return pixels to their status at a particular state in the History palette. Click in the History Brush column in the History palette to set the state to which the Erase to History option returns pixels.

The Magic Eraser

The Magic Eraser tool is grouped with the Eraser tool. Press and hold on the Eraser tool to access the tools in the tool group. You can also use the keyboard shortcut Shift+E to cycle through the Eraser tools.

Use the Magic Eraser tool to erase pixels on a layer to transparency. The Magic Eraser works best when you want to remove the background pixels around a hard-edged object. The Magic Eraser tool erases pixels based on a tolerance level, similar to the way in which the Magic Wand works. (See page 99 for information on the Magic Wand.)

1. To use the Magic Eraser tool, first select the layer on which you want to work. Select the Magic Eraser tool to show the Magic Eraser options in the Options bar. Enter a Tolerance value. Set a low Tolerance value to erase pixels that are very similar in color value to the pixel on which you first click. Set a high Tolerance value to select a wider range of pixels.

Select the Sample All Layers option to erase pixels based on a sample that takes into account color values from all visible layers, not only the currently active layer.

2. Set an Opacity value of 100% to erase pixels completely. Set a lower Opacity value to create a partially transparent effect. Select the Anti-aliased option to create a smoother edge when pixels are erased. (See page 95 for further information on anti-aliasing.)

The Tolerance value extends or limits the number of pixels that are erased.

3. Select Contiguous to erase only pixels that fall within the Tolerance value specified, and that are adjacent to each other. This option erases continuous areas of pixels. Deselect Contiguous if you want the Magic Eraser to erase all pixels that fall within the Tolerance value anywhere in the image.

If you use the Magic Eraser on the Background layer, Photoshop automatically converts the layer to Layer 0.

4. Position the cursor, then click to erase pixels that fall within the Tolerance value.

The Background Eraser

Use the Background Eraser tool when you are working on a layer to erase pixels to transparency. You can set tolerance and sampling values to control the level of transparency and the sharpness of its boundary edges.

1 To erase pixels on a layer, select a layer on which you want to work. Select the Background Eraser tool to show its options in the Options bar. Select a brush from the Brush Presets picker.

The Background Eraser tool displays a crosshair at the center of its brush cursor. This indicates the tool's "hotspot" – the point at which the tool's settings have the greatest effect. The strength of the effect diminishes further away from the hotspot:

2 Choose Contiguous from the Limits pop-up menu to remove adjacent pixels that fall within the tolerance setting. (Discontiguous erases pixels throughout the image, Find Edges preserves sharp edges along objects).

3 Enter a Tolerance value, or drag the Tolerance slider. Set a low Tolerance value to limit the effect to pixels that are very similar in color value to pixels at the "hotspot". Set a high Tolerance value to erase a broader range of similar colors.

4 Choose a Sampling option. Select Continuous to erase all colors that you drag across. Select Once to erase pixels that are the same color as the pixel on which you first click. This is useful when you want to erase areas of solid color. Select Background Swatch to erase areas containing the current background color.

Select the Protect Foreground Color checkbox if you want to prevent the tool from erasing any pixels that match the current foreground color:

☐ Protect Foreground Color

5 Position your cursor, then click or drag to erase pixels on the layer to transparency, based on the settings you have chosen.

The Healing Brush Tools

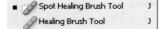

Use the Healing Brush tools to correct flaws and imperfections in an image. The Healing Brush is similar to the Clone Stamp tool in the way it works, but it also matches the texture, luminosity and shading of the sampled pixels to the pixels in the area you want to "heal", producing a smooth, seamless result.

The Spot Healing Brush does not require you to set a sample point. Select a brush size large enough to cover the blemish, position your cursor on the blemish, then click once to remove it. If necessary you can click and drag over the blemish. The Spot Healing brush matches the shading, luminosity, texture and transparency of pixels to remove the unwanted detail.

For the Spot Healing Brush, the Proximity Match option available in the Options bar samples pixels around the tool cursor in order to adjust texture luminosity, shading and transparency values to remove the blemish. Create Texture analyses pixels in the area of the brush to create a texture that replaces the blemish.

1   To "heal" an imperfection, select the Healing Brush tool. Use the Brush Preset Picker palette to choose a brush size. Select a blending mode if required. Use Replace mode to preserve the texture, noise and any film grain at the edges of the brush strokes. Leave the Source option set to Sampled to use pixels from within the image.

2   Select Aligned in the Options bar (see page 85 for information on the Aligned option).

3   Position your cursor on an area of the image that you want to sample from in order to repair the imperfection. Hold down Alt/option, then click the left mouse button. This sets the sample area of pixels.

4   Release the Alt/option key. Move your cursor over the area you want to repair. Click, or press and drag to repair the area. When you click or drag the mouse, the (+) indicates the area of the image you are sampling pixels from.

The Patch Tool

The Patch tool allows you to disguise problems and flaws in an image by cloning or copying pixels from another, similar part of the image. The Patch tool attempts to match the texture and shading of the pixels that are copied or sampled to the source pixels – the pixels you are patching over.

You usually achieve the best results with the Patch tool when you select a relatively small area.

To fix "red eye" caused by camera flash, select the Red Eye tool, position your cursor on the red eye in the image, then click.

In most instances the default settings work well. Adjust Pupil Size and Darken Pupil settings in the Options bar if necessary.

1 Select the Patch tool. Select Source in the Options bar. Drag in the image to select the area of pixels you want to patch over.

2 Still working with the Patch tool, position your cursor inside the Patch selection, then drag the selection area onto the area of the image from which you want to copy pixels.

3 Release the mouse button. The original patch selection is repaired with pixels sampled from the area you released on.

4 Alternatively, select Destination in the Options Bar to reverse the way in which the tool works. Use the Patch tool to select the area of pixels you want to use to make the repair. Drag the Patch selection onto the area of pixels you want to repair. Release the mouse to copy the initial selection area over the flaw.

Color Replacement

Use the Color Replacement tool to paint over specific colors in an image.

See Chapter 4, "Image and Color Basics" for information on selecting foreground color.

1   To paint over a color, select the Color Replacement tool. Select a foreground color. Create settings such as Diameter using the Brush Preset picker in the Options bar. Leave Mode set to Color.

Brush: 10 ▾   Mode: Color ▾   Limits: Contiguous ▾   Tolerance: 30% ▸

2   For Sampling, choose Continuous to sample and replace colors continuously as you drag. Choose Once to replace only the target color you first click on. This makes the tool very specific and typically changes only a limited number of pixels. Choose Background Swatch to limit color changes to pixels that are the same color as the Background color.

Leave the Anti-aliased option selected to achieve a smooth edge to the areas where you replace color:

3   From the Limits drop down menu choose Contiguous to color pixels immediately adjacent to the pixels you drag across and that fall within the Tolerance setting. Choose Discontiguous to color pixels anywhere within the brush diameter, even if the pixels are not immediately adjacent to the pixels you drag across. Choose Find Edges to help preserve sharpness along edge detail as you replace color.

Enter a Tolerance amount, or drag the Tolerance slider to set a Tolerance value.
Set a low value to limit changes to pixels that are very similar in color to the pixels at the center of the brush. Set a high value to color a broader range of pixels:

Tolerance: 28% ▸

4   Position your cursor on the pixels you want to change. The Color Replacement tool displays a crosshair at the center of the brush cursor. This indicates the tool's "hotspot" – the point at which the tool's settings have the greatest effect. Click and drag to paint over the pixels.

pattern @ 200% (L...
200%

Making Selections

One of the most important techniques when using Photoshop is making selections. When you make a selection, you are selecting an area of the image to which you want to make changes, and isolating the remainder of the image so that it is not affected by changes. A selection is indicated on-screen by a selection marquee – a dotted line, sometimes referred to as the "marching ants" border.

Covers

The Marquee Selection Tools

The Marquee selection tools allow you to drag with the mouse to make selections. You can make rectangular or elliptical selections by choosing the appropriate tool.

■ [ ] Rectangular Marquee Tool		M
◯ Elliptical Marquee Tool		M
⋯ Single Row Marquee Tool		
▯ Single Column Marquee Tool		

To make a rectangular or oval selection, choose the Rectangular or Elliptical Marquee tool.

Hold down Shift, then click and drag with the Rectangular or Elliptical Marquee tool to create a square or circular selection. Hold down Alt/option to create a selection from the center out. Hold down Alt+Shift, to create a square or circular selection from the center out.

Position your cursor on the image, then click and drag to define the area you want to select. When you release the cursor you will see a dotted rectangular or oval marquee defining the area of the selection.

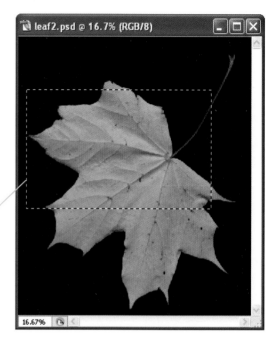

leaf2.psd @ 16.7% (RGB/8)

16.67%

As you are dragging to create a selection, you can hold down the Spacebar to reposition the marquee.

You can reposition the selection marquee if you need to. Make sure the Marquee tool is still selected, position your cursor inside the selection marquee (the cursor changes shape), then click and drag. You can move selection marquees with any of the Selection tools.

With the Marquee tool selected, you can deselect a selection by clicking inside or outside the selection marquee. Alternatively, you can choose Select>Deselect (Ctrl/Command+D).

Marquee Options

You can use the Marquee Options bar to make changes to the way in which the Marquee tools work.

1 Select the Rectangular or Elliptical Marquee tool. Make sure the New Selection button is selected in the Options bar.

2 Use the Style pop-up to create settings for making proportional selections, or selections of a fixed size. If you select Fixed Size, enter the values you require in the Width and Height entry boxes.

3 The Anti-aliased option is an important control when using bitmap applications such as Photoshop. Select Anti-aliased to create a slightly blurred, soft edge around the selection and the pixels that surround the selection. Using Anti-aliased helps avoid creating unwanted jagged edges.

4 Use the Feather entry box to create a soft, feathered edge. (See page 100 in this chapter.)

Moving Selected Pixels

You can use the Selection tools to reposition a selection border, but you must use the Move tool if you want to move pixels from one location to another.

With the Marquee, Lasso or Magic Wand tool selected, position your cursor inside the selection marquee, then hold down Ctrl/Command. The cursor changes temporarily to the Move tool cursor. Click and drag to move the selected pixels.

1 Make a selection. Select the Move tool, then position your cursor inside the Marquee selection border. Click and drag to move the selected pixels.

To move the selection in increments of one pixel with the Move tool selected, press the up, down, left or right arrow keys. Hold down Shift and press the arrow keys to move the selection in increments of five pixels.

When you move pixels on the Background layer, the area from which the pixels are moved fills with the current background color. As long as the selection border remains selected, you can continue to move the pixels. Whilst the selection is active, the pixels in the selection "float" above the underlying pixels, without replacing them.

2 To "defloat" the pixels so that they replace the underlying pixels, choose Select>Deselect if you have the Move tool or Magic Wand tool selected. If you used Ctrl/Command with a Marquee or Lasso tool selected, click outside the selection marquee. As soon as you deselect, the pixels on the Background layer that were underneath the floating selection – the underlying pixels – are completely replaced by the pixels in the floating selection.

In a bitmap image, you cannot have an area where there are no pixels. When you move pixels using the Move tool, the area that was originally selected fills with the current background color.

3 To move a selection and make a copy of it at the same time, hold down Alt/option before you drag with the Move tool. The cursor turns into a double-headed arrow, indicating that you are copying the selection.

With a selection tool selected, position your cursor inside a selection marquee, hold down Ctrl/Command+Alt/option, then click and drag to move a copy of the selected pixels.

4 You can turn a "floating" selection into a layer by choosing Layer>New>Layer Via Cut/Layer Via Copy. (See Chapter 8.)

The Lasso Tools

You can use the Lasso tool to make freeform selections by clicking and dragging. It is a useful tool for selecting irregular areas and for quickly adding to or subtracting from selections made with the Magic Wand tool.

Hold down Shift, then click and drag around an area to add it to the selection. Hold down Alt/option, then click and drag around an area to remove it from the selection.

Select the Lasso tool. Set Feather and Anti-aliased options. Position your cursor on the image. The cursor changes to the Lasso cursor. Click and drag around the part of the image you want to select. Make sure your cursor comes back to the start point. If you release before reaching the start point, Photoshop completes the selection with a straight line. A dotted marquee defines the selected area.

When you return to the start point with the Polygon Lasso tool, a small circle appears at the bottom right of the cursor to indicate that you can close the selection by clicking once.

Polygon Lasso tool

The Polygon Lasso tool creates a freeform selection with straight line segments.

Select the Polygon Lasso tool. Position your cursor on the image, then click; move the cursor, then click… and so on, until you have defined the area you want to select. Click back at the start point to complete the selection. Alternatively, you can double-click to close the selection marquee.

If you have a Feather amount set in the Lasso Options bar, you will not end up with sharp corners on the selection you make.

The Magnetic Lasso tool

The Magnetic Lasso tool is most useful when you want to select an object or an area of the image which contrasts strongly with the area surrounding it.

You cannot use the Magnetic Lasso tool in 32-bit per channel images.

Select the Magnetic Lasso tool. Click on the edge of the object you want to select to place the first fastening point. Either, move

Click on the edge of the shape if you need to add a fastening point manually.

the cursor along the edge of the object, or click and drag along the edge to draw a freehand segment. As you move along the edge of the object, the "active" segment of the selection border snaps to the most clearly defined edge in the image near the cursor. Fastening points are added automatically, at intervals, as you drag.

The Magnetic Lasso tool adds fastening points at intervals as you drag the cursor to create the selection. Fastening points anchor the selection border in place as you create the selection, but disappear when you close the selection border.

2 To close the selection border, position your cursor on the start point, (a small circle at the cursor indicates that you are on the start point) then click. Alternatively, double-click, or press the Enter/ Return key. Photoshop creates a segment from the point you have reached to the start point of the selection border. To close the selection border with a straight line segment, hold down Alt/option and double-click.

Lasso Width

The Magnetic Lasso tool detects edges within the specified distance from the pointer. Enter a value between 1–40.

Frequency

This setting determines the rate at which fastening points are set. Enter a value between 0–100. Set higher values to place fastening points at more frequent intervals.

If the object you want to select has high contrast (i.e. well defined edges) use higher Lasso Width and Edge Contrast settings. For objects with less well defined edges, use lower Lasso Width and Edge Contrast settings.

Edge Contrast

Enter a value between 1–100%. This value determines how sensitive the Magnetic Lasso tool is to edges in the image. Higher values select edges that contrast strongly with their background. Lower values select edges that have smaller amounts of contrast.

Width:	10 px	Edge Contrast:	10%	Frequency:	57	

The Magic Wand Tool

The Magic Wand tool selects continuous areas of color in an image, based on a tolerance setting. Low tolerance settings create a very limited selection of color. Higher settings select a wider range of pixels. The tool is good for selecting areas of reasonably consistent color.

To add to a selection using the Magic Wand tool, hold down Shift, then click on an unselected part of the image.

1 Before creating a selection using the Magic Wand tool, check the Tolerance setting. Double-click the Magic Wand tool to display the Magic Wand Options bar if it is not showing, or choose Window>Options to show the Options bar. Enter a Tolerance value from 0–255. If you set a tolerance value of 255, you will select every pixel in the image.

2 Click on the image to select pixels of similar color value. All adjacent pixels that are within the Tolerance range are selected. Adjust the default setting of 32 as necessary to make the selection you require.

Typically, you fine-tune Magic Wand selections using a combination of the other selection tools, together with the Grow and Similar commands.

3 Deselect the Contiguous option to select pixels throughout the image that fall within the Tolerance setting. The result is similar to using the Similar command (see page 102.)

You cannot use the Magic Wand tool in Bitmap mode.

4 To deselect a selection marquee when the Magic Wand tool is selected, click inside the selection marquee. If you click outside the selection marquee, you create another selection based around the pixel where you clicked.

Feathering Selections

You can define a feathered edge when you make selections using the Lasso tools and the Rectangular or Elliptical Marquee tools.

You can use the Feather option to control the degree to which the edge of a selection is softened or faded. Feathering a selection creates a transition boundary between the selection and the surrounding pixels, which can cause a loss of detail.

1. Select one of the Lasso tools, or the Rectangular or Elliptical Marquee selection tool. In the Options bar, set a Feather value, e.g. 10. The amount you set depends on the effect you want to achieve. Use higher values on high resolution images. Alternatively, using any of the selection tools, you can make a selection and then choose Select>Feather. Enter a value in the Feather Radius box.

Get into the habit of checking for Feather settings in the Options bar before you make a selection so that you don't create a feathered selection unintentionally.

When you set a feather amount, the selection you make may appear more "rounded" than you expect. This is caused by the Feather value.

2. Create a selection using a selection tool. When you move the selection, using the Move tool, you will see the feathered edge around the selection and also where you move the selection from.

Creating a vignette

You can use the feathering option to create a vignette, or soft, fading edge to an image.

Before you make a selection for a vignette effect, make sure you set the background color to white (see page 61).

1. Set a Feather value in the Options bar for the selection tool you are using. Next, create a selection, which can be a regular or irregular shape. Choose Select>Inverse. This reverses the selection – selecting all the pixels that were previously not selected. Press Delete (Mac) or Backspace (Windows) to delete the area surrounding your selection, leaving a feathered edge.

Feathering, unlike anti-aliasing, blurs the inside and outside of a selection boundary.

Modifying Selections

There are many instances when you need to add to or subtract from a selection. You can use any combination of selection tools to make the selection you want. For example, you might start by making a selection with the Magic Wand tool, then add to the selection using the Lasso tool.

1   To add to an existing selection, hold down the Shift key, then click and drag to create another selection marquee that intersects the existing selection marquee.

2   You can use the same technique to create non-adjoining selections. Although the selections may be in different parts of the image, they count and act as one selection. For example, if you apply a filter, the effect will be apparent in all the selection marquees.

3   To add to a selection, hold down Shift and use the Lasso tool to quickly loop around small areas that the Magic Wand tool typically misses out from its selection.

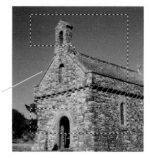

4   To subtract from a selection, hold down Alt/option, then click and drag with a selection tool to intersect the existing selection marquee. The area defined by the intersecting marquee is removed from the original selection.

The Grow and Similar Commands

If necessary, change the Tolerance setting for the Magic Wand tool, before using the Grow command, to achieve a more, or less, inclusive result.

The Grow and Similar commands are very useful when used in conjunction with the Magic Wand tool to add to a selection. Both work according to the Tolerance value set in the Magic Wand Options bar.

The Grow command selects contiguous or adjoining areas of color based on the Tolerance setting in the Magic Wand Options bar.

1 Make a selection. Check that the Tolerance setting in the Magic Wand Options bar is appropriate.

2 Choose Select>Grow to add pixels to the existing selection which fall within the Tolerance setting and are adjacent to pixels already in the selection.

Using the Magic Wand tool, with Contiguous in the Options bar deselected, is the equivalent of using the Similar command.

The Similar command selects non-adjacent pixels that fall within the same Tolerance setting as set in the Magic Wand Options bar.

1 Make a selection using any of the selection tools. Check that the Tolerance setting in the Magic Wand Options bar is appropriate.

2 Choose Select>Similar to select pixels throughout the image that fall within the Tolerance setting.

Pasting Into Selections

Pasting into selections is useful for compositing images.

Create a selection in the destination window.

2 Open the source document, then make the selection you want to paste into the destination document. Choose Edit>Copy to copy the selection to the Clipboard.

3 Click in the destination image window. The selection should still be active. Choose Edit>Paste Into (Ctrl/Command+Shift+V) to paste the Clipboard selection into the selected area.

4 Use the Move tool to reposition the pasted selection relative to the original selection.

5 The Paste Into command creates a layer mask. The layer is active, indicated by the highlight border on the thumbnail in the Layers palette, which means that you can edit the layer. To edit the mask, click the Mask icon in the Layers palette. The highlight border appears on the mask to indicate that the layer mask is selected.

Filling a Selection

See pages 79-81 for a description of the blending modes.

You can use the Fill dialog box in order to fill an entire layer or a selection.

1 To fill a selection, first define either a foreground or background color that you want to fill with, then make a selection. Choose Edit>Fill. Use the Use pop-up to choose the fill type. You can also set Opacity for the fill and a Blending Mode. Click OK.

If you don't make a selection before you choose the Fill command, you fill the entire layer.

2 To fill a selection with a pattern, first define the pattern by making a selection, then choosing Edit>Define Pattern.

3 Make the selection you want to fill with the previously defined pattern.

4 Choose Edit>Fill. Choose Pattern from the Use pop-up. Use the Custom Pattern pop-up menu to access the pattern library. Select a pattern. OK the dialog box to fill the selection with the pattern.

Copying and Pasting Selections

You can use the Clipboard to copy and paste selections within the same image and into other images. You can also drag selections between images.

1 To copy a selection, first make a selection using any of the selection tools. Choose Edit>Copy.

2 To paste the selection into the same image, choose Edit>Paste. The selection is pasted into the image on its own layer. (For information on working with layers, see Chapter Eight, "Layers".)

3 To paste the selection into another image that is already open, click on the other image window to make it active. Choose Edit>Paste to paste the selection from the Clipboard onto a new layer in the active image.

4 You can also drag a selection from one image window into another. You need two image windows open – the source and the destination windows. Make a selection in the source window, select the Move tool, position your cursor within the selection, then click and drag into the destination window. The selection appears on its own layer.

Transforming Selections

The ability to transform a selection's bounding box enables you to fine tune selections, distort selections and make selections that were previously difficult to achieve.

1   To transform a selection, choose Select>Transform Selection. A bounding box with eight handles appears around the selection. A Point of Origin marker appears at the center of the bounding box.

2   To scale a selection, click and drag a handle. The cursor becomes a bi-directional arrow. To scale a selection in proportion, hold down Shift then drag a handle.

3   To rotate a selection, position your cursor just outside the selection border. The cursor changes to a bi-directional, curved arrow. Click and drag in a circular direction.

4   To distort the selection boundary, hold down Ctrl/Command then drag a corner handle.

5   To create a perspective effect on the selection border, hold down Ctrl/Command+Alt/option+Shift, then drag a corner handle.

6   To shear a selection border, hold down Ctrl/Command, then click and drag a center top/bottom or center left/right handle.

7   Click the Cancel button in the Options bar to remove the transform bounding box without applying the changes. Click the Commit button to apply the transformation.

Layers

Layers introduce a considerable degree of flexibility into the way in which you can work with images. Layers let you keep various image elements separate so that you can make changes to the pixels on one layer without affecting pixels on any other layer.

Each additional layer you create increases the file size of the image. You can selectively merge layers into each other to help manage and consolidate layers as you work. When you finish editing your image, you can flatten the image to merge all layers into a single Background layer. You need to do this, for example, to use your image in QuarkXPress. You can save images with layers in Photoshop and TIFF file formats.

Covers

Working with Layers

When you create or open an image for the first time, it consists of one default layer called Background.

1 To create a new layer, choose New Layer from the palette menu. Enter a name for the new layer in the name entry box. You can also choose Opacity and Blending Mode settings at this stage if required.

2 Alternatively, click once on the New Layer icon at the bottom of the Layers palette to create a new layer with default settings. Hold down Alt/option, then click the New Layer icon to access the New Layer dialog box.

3 OK the dialog box. This creates a new, empty layer, which appears in the Layers palette above the previously active layer. Notice also that the file size in the Document Sizes status bar area increases when you paint on or add pixels to the layer.

4 To name a layer, position your cursor on the layer's label, then double-click. Enter a new name in the label entry area, then press Enter/Return on the keyboard.

5 To delete the active layer, choose Delete Layer from the palette menu. Click Yes or No in the delete warning box. Or, drag the Layer name onto the Wastebasket icon at the bottom of the Layers palette. No warning alert appears if you use this method.

You can click the Eye icon to hide/show a layer group and also a layer style.

Selecting, hiding and showing layers

You can only paint, edit pixels or make color adjustments to one layer at a time. This is often referred to as the "target" or active layer.

Click on the layer name in the Layers palette to make it active. The layer name highlights to indicate that it is active. The name of the active layer appears in the title bar of the image window.

`abstract2-1.psd @ 100% (ellipse-small, RGB/8)`

To select all pixels on a layer, hold down Ctrl/ Command and click on the layer name in the Layers palette.

To hide the contents of a layer, click on the Eye icon in the leftmost column of the Layers palette. To show a layer, click in the leftmost column to bring back the Eye icon.

Reordering layers

You cannot change the stacking order of the Background layer, but it is often necessary to change the stacking order of other layers to control which layers appear in front of other layers.

You can move pixels in a layer beyond the edge of your picture. These non-visible pixels are saved with the document. Non-visible pixels are lost when you flatten the image.

To change the layering order, click and drag the layer name you want to reposition. Notice the horizontal bar that appears as you move the layer upwards or downwards. Release the mouse when the horizontal bar appears in the position to which you want the layer moved.

Repositioning layer contents

You can reposition the entire contents of a layer using the Move tool.

You can nudge the contents of a selected layer in 1-pixel increments by pressing the arrow keys when the Move tool is selected.

Click on the layer you want to move in the Layers palette. Select the Move tool, then position your cursor anywhere on the image. Click and drag to move the layer.

Merging and Flattening Layers

The Merge Visible Layers command in the palette menu merges only the currently visible layers.

Use the Merge commands to combine two or more layers into one layer. This is useful for keeping the file size down and for consolidating elements on different layers into a single manageable layer or unit.

1. To merge all the visible layers in your document, first hide any layers you don't want to merge. Make sure one of the layers you want to merge is active, then choose Merge Visible from the palette menu, or choose Layer>Merge Visible.

When you use the Flatten Image command, any hidden layers are discarded.

2. To merge a layer with the layer below it, first select the layer, then choose Merge Down from the palette menu, or choose Layer>Merge Down.

When you convert images between some modes you are prompted to flatten the file. Make sure you save a copy of the file first if you want to be able to go back and make further changes to the layers.

Flattening images

When you flatten an image, you end up with a Background layer only. This reduces the file size. Flatten an image when you have finished creating and positioning the elements of your composite image, and are ready to save the file in a suitable format for placing in a page layout application.

To flatten an image, make sure that all the layers you want to keep are visible. Choose Flatten Image from the Layers palette menu, or choose Layers>Flatten Image.

Moving Layers Between Images

You can copy a complete layer from one Photoshop document to another, similar to the way you move a selection from one document to another.

The layer you move into the destination image window is rendered at the resolution of that window. This may cause the elements on the moved layer to appear larger or smaller than in the original window. To avoid surprises, make sure that the source and destination images are at the same resolution. Also, if the modes of the two images are different, the layer you move is converted to match the mode of the destination window.

1 First make sure you have two document windows open – a "source" document and a "destination" document. The source document contains the layer you want to copy. The destination document is the document into which you want to copy the layer.

2 Click in the source document window to make it active. Position your cursor on the layer in the Layers palette, then drag the layer you want to copy from the source document into the destination document window. A bounding box indicates the layer you are copying.

If necessary, use the Defringe command (Layer>Matting> Defringe) to remove any fringe around pixels on a layer that you copy from one image to another.

3 Position the layer and then release the mouse. The layer is positioned above the previously active layer in the destination document's Layers palette. The destination document becomes the active image window.

Selecting and Linking Layers

The principle of linking layers works, even if the layers are not next to each other in the Layers palette.

Linking or multiple selection of layers is useful when you want to keep elements of an image on separate layers, but you need to make changes to them as a unit.

Choose Select>All Layers to select all layers in an image; choose Select>Deselect All Layers to have no layer selected.

Select a specific type of layer, such as a Shape or Type layer, then choose Select>Select Similar Layers to select all layers of that type in the image.

Use the Move tool to reposition the elements on the linked layers as one.

Selecting multiple layers creates a temporary grouping that allows you to manipulate two or more layers as a unit. Linking layers keeps the layers grouped until you unlink them. You can move, align and transform multiple selected layers or linked layers, and also apply styles from the Styles palette.

1 To select multiple, consecutive layers, select the first layer, hold down Shift, then click the last layer in the range. To select multiple, non-consecutive layers, select the first layer, hold down Ctrl/Command, then click each layer you want to add to the selection.

2 To remove a multiple selection of layers, click on any individual layer in the Layers palette. Or, click in an empty area below the bottom-most layer in the palette.

3 To link layers, select two or more consecutive, or non-consecutive layers. Then click the Link button ( ) at the bottom of the Layers palette. A link icon appears to the right of a linked layer. When you select a linked layer in the Layers palette, all other layers linked to it display a link icon to indicate their linked status.

4 To unlink a single layer, select the specific layer you want to unlink, then click the Link button. Other layers in a set of linked layers remain linked.

5 To unlink all layers in a link set, either select each link manually, or select one linked layer, then choose Layer>Select Linked Layers. Click the Link button to unlink all linked layers.

Locking Layers

There are four levels of lock that can be applied to layers. A dimmed lock icon appears to the right of the layer when you select one of the lock options. A solid lock icon appears when the layer is fully locked.

1 To completely lock a layer, select the layer in the Layers palette, then click the Lock All option. You will not be able to reposition the layer or make any changes to it, including changing blending mode, opacity and layer style.

2 To prevent the layer from being moved using the Move tool, click the Lock Position option.

3 To disable painting tools on the layer, select the Lock Image pixels option. You can still edit any mask applied to the layer and you can move the layer. Selecting the Lock Image pixels option automatically locks transparency for the layer.

4 Click Lock Transparency to preserve transparent areas of a layer.

You can make changes to the existing pixels on the layer, but you cannot make changes to any areas of transparency. For example, if Lock Transparency is selected, the blur filters do not work effectively on the layer as pixels cannot spread into the areas of transparency to create the blur effect.

Adjustment Layers

An adjustment layer is created above the currently active layer. It's settings apply to the layers below it and do not affect layers above.

Using an adjustment layer is like positioning a lens above the pixels on the layers below it to change their appearance. If you don't like the result, you can edit the adjustment layer to achieve the result you want, or you can discard it. When you are satisfied with the result you can implement the adjustment layer as a permanent change.

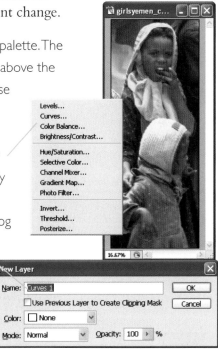

Select a layer in the Layers palette. The adjustment layer is created above the currently active layer. Choose Layer>New Adjustment Layer. Choose a type from the New Adjustment Layer sub-menu. This automatically becomes the name for the layer. In the New Layer dialog box, enter a different name if desired. Set Opacity and Blending Mode at this stage if you want to. Click OK.

You can restack adjustment layers as any other layer.

You can copy and paste adjustment layers between images in order to apply consistent color and tonal changes to different images.

As an alternative, you can click the New Adjustment Layer button ( ) at the bottom of the Layers palette, then choose an adjustment layer type.

By reducing the Opacity setting for an adjustment layer you can lessen the effect of the settings you create in the adjustment layer dialog box.

Depending on the type of adjustment layer you chose, the appropriate dialog box opens. Create the settings you want to experiment with. OK the dialog box.

4 The new adjustment layer appears in the Layers palette as the active layer. The settings you create now apply to all layers below the adjustment layer.

Create a selection before you create an adjustment layer to limit the effects of the adjustment layer settings to a specific area of an image:

5 Click the Eye icon to hide/show the preview of the changes brought about by the adjustment layer settings. Double-click the adjustment layer to re-enter the appropriate adjustment dialog box to make changes to the settings.

You can apply adjustment layer settings to specific areas of an image by editing the adjustment layer image mask:

See page 156 for information on editing layer masks.

6 Drag the adjustment layer into the Wastebasket if you want to discard the settings.

7 When you are ready to make the settings of the adjustment layer permanent, either use one of the Merge commands from the palette menu, or flatten the image.

The adjustment layer settings do not have a permanent effect on pixels until the layer is merged with other layers, or the image is flattened.

Layer Groups

When you create complex images with multiple layers it is convenient to simplify the layers palette by combining related layers together into a layer group. Creating layer groups in complex, multi-layered images makes it much easier to manage the elements in the image.

In the New Group from Layers dialog box, leave the Mode option set to Pass Through to ensure that blending and opacity settings apply to all layers in an image and are not limited to the layers in the layer set.

1 To create a new layer set, click the New Layer Set button in the bottom of the Layers palette to use the current default settings, or choose New Layer Set from the palette menu.

2 To create a layer group from existing layers, first select the layers you want to combine into a layer group. Choose New Group From Layers in the palette menu ( ), or choose Layer>New>Group from Layers.

To nest a layer group within another layer group, drag the layer group you want to nest onto an existing layer group folder.

3 To move a layer into a layer group, drag it onto the Layer Group folder. Release the mouse when the Layer Group folder highlights. The layer is positioned at the bottom of the layers already in the layer group. If the layer group is expanded, drag the layer to the desired position. Release when the highlight bar is in the correct position.

4 Click the Collapse/Expand triangle to reveal or hide the layers contained within the layer group.

Layer Styles

Each layer style provides a range of options specific to that style. Experiment with the options to achieve the effect you want.

Using the Layer Style sub-menu, you can create sophisticated layer effects such as soft shadows, beveled and embossed edges, and inner and outer glows quickly and easily. This example consists of 3 layers – a white Background layer, a colored circle Shape layer and a colored triangle Shape layer, and uses Bevel and Emboss options to demonstrate the principles for creating a layer style.

1   To apply a layer style, click on a layer in the Layers palette to make it active. Choose Layer>Layer Style>Bevel & Emboss.

In the Layer Style dialog box, make sure the Preview option is selected to see the effect applied in the image.

2   In the Structure section, choose a style from the Style pop-up menu and a technique from the Technique pop-up menu. Select the Up/Down radio button to light the effect from above or below.

3   Use the Depth entry box or slider to adjust the height of the effect. Use the Size slider to control the spread of the bevel. The Soften slider controls the

You cannot apply a layer style to the Background layer, a layer set or a locked layer.

overall intensity of the effect and helps reduce irregularities or artifacts in the effect, creating a smoother result.

You can also select a layer style option using the Add Layer Style button ( ) at the bottom of the Layers palette.

4   In the Shading area, enter a value in the Angle entry box to control the

direction of the light source. Enter a value in the Altitude entry box to define the apparent depth of the light source. Drag in the Angle/Altitude disk to create settings manually if you prefer.

5 Gloss Contour allows you to change the transition of the effect across the affected pixels on the layer.

6 Adjust settings for the Highlight and Shadow edges of the effect.

It is a good idea initially to leave the blending modes set to Screen and Multiply respectively. Experiment with the Opacity sliders to create a more subtle effect.

Click on the Expand/Collapse triangle to hide or show the layer styles applied to a layer:

7 OK the dialog when you are satisfied with the results. Notice in the Layers palette a "f" symbol (🄵) on the layer, indicating that there is a layer effect applied to the layer. Whilst the "f" symbol appears the layer effect remains editable.

Click the Eye icon to the left of the layer effect to control its visibility:

Managing Layer Styles

Once you have created a layer effect you can continue to edit the effect and you can use a variety of commands from the Layer Effects sub-menu to manage the effects.

1 To edit the layer effect settings, select the layer, then click the Expand triangle to display layer effects as separate entries in the Layers palette. Double-click the name of the effect you want to edit. You can continue to adjust settings as often as you need to achieve the desired result.

To temporarily disable layer effects on all layers, not just the active layer, choose Layer>Layer Style>Hide All Effects. Choose Layer>Layer Style>Show All Effects to reverse the process.

2 To keep the angle of the light source constant if you are using layer effects on more than one layer in an image, choose Layer>Layer Style>Global Light. Enter a value for the Angle in the Angle entry box. OK the dialog box. Make sure you select the Use Global Light checkbox when you create multiple layer effects in the Layer Style dialog box.

3 To copy exact layer effect settings from one layer to another, first select a layer with a layer effect applied to it, then choose Copy Layer Style from the Layer Style sub-menu. Click on another layer in the Layers palette. Choose Paste Layer Style from the Layer Style sub-menu.

Once you merge a layer with a layer effect applied to it, you can no longer adjust the layer effect settings.

4 To permanently remove layer styles from a layer, make sure you select the appropriate layer, then choose Layer>Layer Style>Clear Layer Styles.

5 Layer styles automate procedures that in the past you had to perform yourself. Use the Create Layer command from the Layer Styles sub-menu to separate the layer effect into the multiple layers that Photoshop uses to create the effect. This can be useful if you need to edit specific parts of the effect.

Transforming Layers

Once you have moved pixels to a new layer you can then transform the layer. Using Free Transform you can scale, rotate, distort, skew and create perspective effects.

1   Ensure the layer is active. Choose Edit>Free Transform. A bounding box with handles appears around the pixels. To scale a layer, drag a handle. To scale in proportion, hold down Shift then drag a corner handle.

2   To rotate a layer, position your cursor slightly outside the bounding box. The cursor changes to a bi-directional arrow. Drag in a circular direction. You can drag the Point of Origin marker to a new position to specify the point around which the rotation takes place.

3   To skew the layer, hold down Ctrl/ Command+Shift, then drag the center top/bottom, or the center left/right handle.

4   To create perspective, hold down Ctrl/ Command+Alt/option+Shift then drag a corner handle. To distort the layer, hold down Ctrl/Command then drag a corner handle. This allows you to move corner handles independently.

5   Click the Cancel button in the Options bar, or press Esc to revert to the original state without making changes. Click the Commit button or press Return/Enter to accept the transformation and remove the Transformation bounding box.

New Layer Commands

The New Layer via Cut (Ctrl/Command+Shift+J) and the New Layer via Copy (Ctrl/Command+J) commands are essential options when creating layers. Use these commands to either cut or copy selected pixels to a new layer.

1. Start by making a selection. Then choose Layer>New>Layer via Copy to create a new layer containing a copy of the selected pixels. The new layer is automatically named Layer 1, etc, depending on the number of layers already in the document. The new layer is created above the layer that is active when you choose the Layer via Copy command.

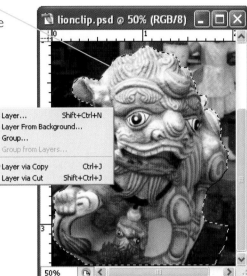

2. Make a selection, then choose New Layer via Cut to cut the selected pixels to a new layer. Notice when you reposition the

pixels on the new layer, the area on the Background layer from which they were cut is filled with the current background color.

Layer Comps

A layer comp is a snapshot of an image that records the visibility and position of layers, and any layer styles for an image at a particular point in time. Layer comps provide a convenient means for recording various permutations of image layers without having to create multiple, separate image files. Unlike Snapshots created in the History palette, Layer comps are saved with the file.

See page 27 for information on working with palettes in the Palette Well.

1. On launching Photoshop, the Layer Comps palette is docked in the Palette Well in the Options bar. Click the Layer Comps tab to work with the palette from the dock.

Position your cursor on the Layer Comp tab in the Palette Well, then drag into the Photoshop working area to create a floating palette. Choose Dock to Palette Well from the Layer Comps palette menu (⊙) if you want to move the palette back to the Palette Well.

2. Create the arrangement and visibility settings for the layer palette that you want to record, then either click the Create New Layer Comp button (🔲) at the bottom of the palette, or choose New Layer Comp from the palette menu.

3. In the New Layer Comp dialog box, enter a name for the Layer Comp. Select Visibility, Position and Appearance options that you want to record in the Layer Comp.

4. Add an additional explanatory note in the Comment entry box if required.

Settings you create in the New Layer Comp dialog box become the defaults for the next time you use the dialog box.

5. Click OK. The New Layer Comp is added at the bottom of the Layer Comps palette, below any existing Layer Comps.

Viewing and Managing Layer Comps

Layer Comps add flexibility and a degree of complexity to the way in which you work with and manage images. You should be careful about the way you manage layer comp variations in order to work effectively, smoothly and productively.

1 To change the name of a layer comp, double-click the layer comp name in the Layer Comp palette to highlight the existing name. Enter a new name then press Return/Enter.

2 To change the layer comp settings you selected when you first created the layer comp, double-click the layer comp entry line (but not directly on the layer comp name) to access the Layer Comp Options dialog box. Make changes as required.

3 To display a layer comp in the image window, either click in the Apply Layer Comp box to the left of the layer comp name, or click the Apply Previous/ Next Selected Layer Comp arrow button at the bottom of the palette.

4 Click the Apply Last
Document State box,
or choose Restore Last
Document State from the

palette menu to return to the state of the document you are
currently working on.

5 If you make changes to a layer, for example, deleting a layer that
is already recorded as an element in a Layer Comp, a warning
triangle appears to the right of all layer comps that are affected.
You can update the
layer comp with
the new settings by

*Layer Comps add
to the file size
of an image. It is
a good idea to
delete at least
some of your layer comps when
they are no longer required.*

selecting the layer
comp, then clicking
the Update Layer
Comp button (   ),
or choosing Update
Layer Comp from the
palette menu.

6 To delete a layer comp, click on it to select it, then click the
Wastebasket icon at the bottom of the palette, or drag the layer
comp into the Wastebasket. There is no warning message when
you delete a layer comp. Use the History palette if necessary to
restore a deleted layer comp.

Smart Objects

Smart Objects provide enhanced flexibility as you work in Photoshop as they can be edited outside the parent file as independent components. Also, you can make repeated edits and transformations to Smart Objects without degrading image quality. You can import vector Smart Objects from Adobe Illustrator, or you can create Smart Objects from selected layers within Photoshop.

Vector Smart Objects from Illustrator

Pasting or placing Illustrator artwork as a vector Smart Object allows you to make multiple, non-destructive changes to the artwork in Photoshop. Photoshop achieves this by retaining a link to the original Illustrator artwork which it then continues to reference as you edit and transform it.

1 Working in Illustrator, select the artwork you want to use as a Smart Object in Photoshop. Choose Edit>Copy to copy the artwork to the clipboard.

2 Launch Photoshop. Choose Edit>Paste. In the Paste dialog box select the Smart Object radio button. Click OK.

3 The Illustrator artwork appears in a bounding box in the center of the screen area. Position your cursor inside the bounding box, then click and drag to reposition the object if necessary. Drag bounding box handles to scale the artwork to the required size. Hold down Shift, then drag a corner handle to scale the object in proportion.

4 Click the Commit button in the options bar when you are ready to place the object on a new layer as a Smart Object. Or, press enter on the keyboard. The object creates

a Vector Smart Object layer. The Smart Object icon appears in the layer thumbnail in the Layers palette to indicate that it is a Smart Object layer.

5 To edit the original Smart Object element in Illustrator either double-click the Vector Smart Object thumbnail, or, make sure the layer is active then choose Edit Contents from the Layer palette menu. A warning dialog box reminds you to save any changes you make in Illustrator so that the Photoshop document updates accordingly when you return to it.

Smart Objects from Photoshop Layers

1 To create a Smart Object from existing Photoshop layers, first select two or more layers. Choose Group into New Smart Object from the Layer palette menu. The selected layers convert to a single Smart Object layer.

2 To edit the Smart Object layer as an independent file, double-click the Smart Object layer thumbnail. A warning message reminds you to choose File>Save to commit any changes you make to the external Smart Object.

3 To return to the parent Photoshop document and update it with changes made to the Smart Object externally, close the Smart Object window. Click save if prompted.

Warping

Warping is a type of transformation that allows you to bend objects on layers to create interesting effects, or to map objects to curved surfaces. You can create custom warp effects manually, or you can choose from a variety of warp styles which you can then customize to meet your requirements.

You cannot apply Warp transformations to Vector Smart Object layers.

1 To warp a selected layer, choose Edit>Transform>Warp. A default warp mesh appears on the contents of the layer.

2 To manually create a custom warp effect, you can drag any of the warp gridlines, drag within any of the mesh segments, or you can drag any of the corner anchor points, or direction points that appear around the

You can use Edit>Undo to undo the last custom warp adjustment.

edge of the warp mesh.

These direction points function in the same way as direction points on a curve segment of a path (see Chapter 10 for further details).

Using Warp presets

1 To warp a selected layer using a preset style, choose Edit>Transform>Warp.

2 Select a warp preset from the Warp style pop-up menu.

3   To customize the preset warp style, either drag the Bend anchor point which appears on the warp mesh, or enter a value in the Bend entry box in the Options bar.

4   In the Options bar you can enter values in the H entry box (-100–100) to apply horizontal distortion. Enter a value in the V entry box (-100–100) to apply vertical distortion.

Click the Switch Warp button in the Options bar to switch from a warp mesh to a standard free transform bounding box or vice versa:

5   Click the Change Warp Orientation button in the Options bar to apply the warp from the opposite orientation.

Working with Type

You can create and edit type directly in the image window. The type you create is preserved as vector outlines or paths which means that Photoshop can output type with sharp, resolution-independent edges.

The Masked Type option allows you to create complex selections in the shape of type characters.

You can choose different alignments vertically and horizontally for type, you can rotate it, fill it with a gradient, pattern or image, create translucent type and much more.

Covers

Chapter Nine

Creating Point Type

You can create two kinds of type: Point type and Paragraph type. Typically, you use Point type when you want to work with small amounts of text, such as a single character, word, or line. Use Paragraph type when you are working with more extensive blocks of type in paragraphs.

The small bar running through the bottom of the I-beam cursor indicates the position of the type's baseline.

1 To create Point type, select the Horizontal Type tool (T). You can create settings for the type using options in the Options bar, or the Character and Paragraph palettes, before you enter the type, or you can format the type after you enter it.

You can also commit type by pressing the Enter key on the numeric keypad, or selecting any other tool in the Toolbox.

2 Position your cursor in the image window, then click to place the text insertion point. Clicking with the Horizontal Type tool takes Photoshop into Text Editing mode.

3 Enter text using the keyboard. You must press Enter (Windows), Return (Mac) on the main keyboard to begin a new line. Point type does not wrap.

You must be in Text Editing mode to enter, edit or format text.

4 Click on the Commit button in the Options bar when you have finished entering or editing type to commit the Type layer. This takes Photoshop out of Text Editing mode and you can now perform other tasks on the image. The type appears on its own layer. Click the Cancel button to discard the type.

For images in Multichannel, Bitmap or Indexed Color mode, type does not appear on its own layer, it appears as pixels on the Background layer and cannot be edited.

Creating Paragraph Type

When you work with Paragraph type, you define the width of the column of text. The text wraps to a new line when it reaches the edge of the type bounding box.

1 To create Paragraph type, select the Horizontal Type tool. You can create settings for the type using options in the Options bar, or the Character and Paragraph palettes before you enter the type, or you can format the type after you enter it.

If you enter more type than can fit in the type bounding box, an overflow symbol appears in the bottom right corner of the bounding box:

```
overset text marker ap-
pears in bottom right of
```

Make the type smaller, or the box bigger, to see all the type.

2 Position your cursor at one corner of the type area you want to create. Drag diagonally to define the size of the type's bounding box.

3 With the Horizontal Type tool selected, you can hold down Alt/option, then click in the image to access the Paragraph Text Size dialog box. Enter values for Width and Height, then click OK.

To resize the type bounding box, select the Horizontal Type tool, click on the Type layer in the Layers palette, then click in the text itself. Drag a resize handle to change the size of the text area.

4 Enter text using the keyboard. Text wraps when it reaches the edge of the type bounding box. Press Enter/Return on the main keyboard only when you want to begin a new paragraph.

This is type that is typed into a bounding box created by pressing and dragging with the Type tool selected. The type wraps when it reaches the edge of the bounding box.

5 Click on the Commit button in the Options bar to accept the Type layer. Or, click the Cancel button to abandon changes. Both buttons take Photoshop out of Text Editing mode and you can now perform other tasks on the image. The type appears on its own layer.

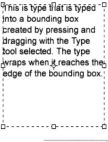

Editing and Selecting Type

If you have any difficulty placing the text insertion point in the text you want to edit, click on the type layer in the Layers palette to activate the layer first.

To edit type you must go into Text Editing mode. To make changes to the character/paragraph formatting of text you must first highlight or select the text on which you want to work. You can then make changes.

Editing text

To edit text select the Horizontal Type tool. Click directly into the text you want to change. This takes Photoshop into Text Editing mode. Make changes using the keyboard as necessary. Click the Commit button in the Options bar to accept the changes you make and to leave Text Editing mode. Click the Cancel button in the Options bar if you do not want to keep the changes.

Editable Type layers are represented by the "T" icon in the Layers palette. Double-click the "T" icon to select all the text on a Type layer:

Selecting text

Make sure you are in Text Editing mode, then click and drag across the text to highlight a specific range of characters, from a single character to a word to all visible text. Double-click on a word to highlight one word. Triple-click to highlight a line of text. Click four times to select a paragraph.

To reposition type, select the Move tool, make sure the Type layer is selected in the Layers palette, then drag the Type layer as you would to reposition any other layer.

2 In Text Editing mode, use Ctrl/Command+A to select all text on the layer, or choose Select>All.

3 With the appropriate range of text highlighted you can then make changes to the settings. The changes you make apply to the highlighted text only.

Character Settings

You can use options in the Options bar when the Type tool is selected, or in the Character palette to change the settings for selected text.

Font

Use the Font pop-up to choose from the list of fonts available on your system. Choose a style – such as Bold or Italic – from the Font Style pop-up.

Size

Enter a value in the Size box to change the size of your type. Points are the default unit of measurement for type in Photoshop.

Leading

Leading controls the distance from one baseline of type to the next. Enter a leading value in points in the Leading entry box. Photoshop applies a default leading value of 120% of the type size you have selected if you leave the leading set to (Auto).

And the nights

that have

come between

Kerning and tracking

In the Character palette, you can create settings for kerning and tracking. Metrics, the default, uses the built-in pair kerning table for the font.

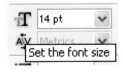

To kern character pairs, click between the characters in the text to place the text insertion bar. You can enter a value in the Kerning entry box or use the pop-up to choose a preset value. Negative values move characters closer together. Positive values move characters apart. Press Enter/Return to accept the changes made in the dialog.

To change the color of selected text, click the Color box in the Options bar or in the Character palette. (See pages 63-64 for further information on using the Color Picker palette.)

2 For Tracking, highlight a range of text you want to track. Enter a value in the Tracking entry box, or use the pop-up.

AWAY

Tracking = 84

AWAY

Tracking = -36

Baseline Shift

The Baseline Shift control allows you to move highlighted characters above or below their original baseline to create a variety of effects.

You must commit or cancel changes to type before proceeding to make other changes to the image.

1 To baseline-shift characters, in Text Editing mode make sure you highlight the characters you want to shift.

2 Enter a positive value to baseline-shift upwards, enter a negative value to baseline-shift downward.

It's a T Y P E

Anti-aliasing

In most instances, fractional character widths provide the best spacing for type. Switch off the Fractional Widths option when working with type below 20 points that is to be viewed on screen. If you leave the option selected, type characters may run together when displayed on a monitor screen.

Access the Fractional Widths option from the Character palette menu ( ).

The anti-aliased setting in the Options bar creates type with a slightly soft edge. It does this by blurring the pixels that form the edge of the type. Use this option to avoid unnecessary jagged edges, unless you are working with very small type. Anti-aliasing text can help the type to blend into its background. Text that is not anti-aliased can look jagged. Choose an amount of anti-aliasing from the Anti-alias pop-up in the Options bar.

Type at very small sizes can appear blurred if anti-aliasing is applied.

Paragraph Settings

With the Type tool selected, you can click the Palettes button ( ) in the Options bar to show the Paragraph palette.

The controls in the Paragraph palette are most useful when you are working with Paragraph type consisting of one or more paragraphs. Choose Window>Paragraph if the palette is not already showing.

Before you can apply Paragraph settings you must highlight the range of text on which you want to work. (See page 132.)

Select the Type layer in the Layers palette to apply settings to all paragraphs on that layer.

Alignment

To change the alignment for selected paragraphs, or a complete layer, click on one of the alignment buttons: Left, Right, Center, in the Paragraph palette or Options bar.

To set an indent in millimeters, enter a number, followed by mm.

Alternatively, choose one of the Justify alignment options to justify type so that both edges of the column are straight. You cannot justify Point type. The variations for justified type affect how the last line of a paragraph is treated. Rest the cursor on the icon for a ToolTip label.

Indents

To set a Left, Right or First Line indent for selected paragraphs, enter a value in the appropriate entry box.

Use the Hyphenate option to allow or disallow hyphenation in selected text:

Space Before, Space After

To create additional space above and/or below a paragraph or range of selected paragraphs, enter a value in the Space Before and/or Space After entry boxes.

Masked Type

In essence, the Masked Type option creates a complex selection – a selection in the shape of type. This can be powerful and flexible when you want to show images through the shape of letterforms.

Before you commit it, you can highlight, format and move mask type as you would standard type.

1 Select the Type Mask tool. Position your cursor on the image where you want the type to start. Click. This sets the text insertion point. A translucent color mask appears across the image.

2 Enter text on the keyboard. As you type the colored mask becomes transparent in the letterforms to indicate the type mask selection. Click the Commit button in the Options bar to create the selection.

After you commit the type mask selection, use one of the selection tools to reposition the selection border if necessary.

3 A type selection appears in the image window. Notice that the Type Mask tool does not create a new layer.

The Masked Type option creates a selection. You can move, copy, fill or stroke the masked type selection as you can for any other selection.

4 You can now drag the selection to a new image window, create a new layer from the selection or use any commands that you would typically use on a selection.

Type and Layer Styles

Layer styles can be applied to type layers whilst the type layer remains an editable type layer.

1 To apply a Layer Style to a type layer, first click on the type layer to make it active.

2 Choose Layer>Layer Styles. Select a style from the style sub-menu. Create settings in the Layer Style dialog box. When you OK the dialog box, the layer in the Layers palette now has a "T" and a "f" icon indicating that it is an editable type layer with a layer effect applied. (See page 117 for information on working with layer styles. See page 131 for information on working with editable type layers.)

The editable type layer with layer style separated from the background layer.

Type Effects

Photoshop provides a variety of creative techniques for producing interesting effects with type.

See Chapter 10 – "Paths" for information on creating paths and working with the Pen and Shape tools.

Type on a path

You can create type that follows a path created using the Pen tool or a Shape tool.

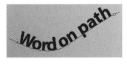

1 Select the Horizontal or Vertical Type tool. Position your cursor on the path. It is important to place the baseline indicator on the path. Click on the path. A text insertion point appears where you click. Begin typing. Click the Commit/Cancel button in the Options bar to accept/discard changes. When you commit type on a path, the type appears on a new layer in the Layers palette.

The baseline indicator is the squiggly line that crosses the I-beam three-quarters of the way down the cursor.

2 To reposition the type along the path, select the Path Selection tool, or the Direct Selection tool. Position your cursor at the beginning of the type. When the cursor changes to the I-beam with arrow ( ), click and drag to move the type along the path.

Warp Type

Photoshop provides a variety of preset type warps that you can customize to suit your requirements.

To flip type across a path, select the Path Selection tool, or the Direct Selection tool. Position your cursor on the type. When the cursor changes to the I-beam with arrow, click and drag the cursor across the path.

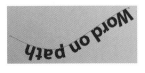

1 To warp type, make sure that you have selected a type layer in the Layers palette. Click the Warp Type button ( ) in the Options bar. Choose a warp preset effect from the Style pop-up menu. Use the Bend, Horizontal and Vertical Distortion sliders to control the effect. Click OK. Warped type remains editable. Choose None from the Style pop-up menu to remove warping from a type layer.

Paths

An understanding of paths in Photoshop is essential for creating cutouts for use in page layout applications such as QuarkXPress and Adobe InDesign. Paths can also be used to create accurate selections.

You can save paths with the image, convert paths into selections, or convert selections into paths. You can also export paths to Adobe Illustrator.

Covers

Chapter Ten

Converting Selections to Paths

A quick technique for creating a path is to make a selection, convert the selection into a work path, and then into a path.

Use Window> Show Paths to show the Paths palette.

1 First make a selection using any of the selection tools. Then, choose Make Work Path from the Paths palette menu.

2 The Make Work Path dialog box appears. Specify a Tolerance value (from 0.5–10).

The Tolerance value controls how closely the path conforms to the selection. A low Tolerance value creates a path that follows the selection tightly, but creates a greater number of points. A high Tolerance value produces a path that follows the selection more loosely, but with fewer points.

3 OK the dialog box. A work path appears in the Paths palette, along with a thumbnail of the path. The selection disappears. Choose Save Path from the pop-up menu if you want to save this path before making any adjustments to it. Enter a name. OK the dialog box. The new path appears in the palette, replacing the work path.

4 To hide the path, click in empty space in the Paths palette. To show the path, click on the path name to select it. The path highlights.

You can only have one work path in the Paths palette at any one time. A work path is a temporary path only. For a path to be saved when you save your file, you must first save the path.

Converting paths to selections

You can also convert a path into a selection. This is useful when you want a very accurate selection.

1 To convert a path into a selection, click on the path in the Paths palette to highlight it. Then choose Make Selection from the palette menu, or click the Load Path as Selection icon.

Using the Pen Tool

You can use the Pen tool to create paths. When you start to create a path it appears as a "work path" in the Paths palette. A work path is only a temporary path.

The Pen tool creates anchor points which are connected by straight lines or curved segments. You can use the other tools in the Paths tool group to modify a path by adding, deleting or moving anchor points, and by changing the nature of the point, from smooth to corner and vice versa. You can also edit curved segments by dragging the Bézier direction points.

Use the Paths palette menu (⊙) to create a new path before you use the Pen tool to automatically save the path without going through the intermediary stage of a work path.

1 To create a path, select the Pen tool

in the Toolbox. Make sure the Create Path icon is selected. You can select the Rubber Band option from the drop down triangle in the Options bar to see a preview of the line segments as you draw.

You can press the Delete key to delete the last anchor point. Press Delete twice to delete the entire path.

2 Position your cursor where you want to start drawing the path, then click, release the button, move the mouse and click again to create a straight line segment. Continue moving your cursor and clicking to create further straight line segments.

3 Alternatively, you can click and drag to set an anchor point and create direction lines for a curve segment. Then, release the button and move the cursor, and again click and drag to create the next anchor point with direction lines. Continue in this way to create the path you want. Position the Pen tool cursor at the start point. Notice the cursor now has a small circle attached to it. Click to create a closed path. The path will appear in the Paths palette with the default title of Work Path.

Use the Freeform Pen tool to create a path by clicking and dragging the mouse. This is similar to drawing with a pencil. You have no control over where Photoshop places anchor points, but you can easily edit the path after it is drawn.

4 To create an open path, follow the techniques outlined in steps 1–3 but instead of clicking back at the start point click on the Pen tool in the Toolbox to finish the path. This is now an open path to which you could, for example, apply a stroke.

Creating corner points

As you use the Pen tool to create paths, you can draw corner points as you go, in combination with straight line segments and smooth points. In many instances, smooth points alone cannot create the shape of the path you want.

Provided that Auto Add/Delete is selected in the Options bar, you can use the Pen tool to add and delete anchor points. The tool cursor changes intelligently, depending on whether you position the cursor on an anchor point or a line segment.

A corner point allows a sharp change of direction at the anchor point. In a corner point, the direction points can be manipulated independently. This is what makes them essential to create paths that require sharp changes of direction.

1 To draw a corner point, click and drag as you would to set a smooth point. Concentrate on getting the shape of the path coming into the point correct. Release the mouse button.

The paths in these illustrations have been moved one pixel away from the edge of the leaf so that they display more clearly. When you create a clipping path, it is best to position the path a pixel or so inside the shape you want to cut out, to avoid unwanted edge pixels being included. Unwanted edge pixels are sometimes referred to as "edge tear".

2 Position your cursor on the anchor point, hold down Alt/option, then click and drag off the point. This converts the point to a corner point. You are now controlling the direction of the outgoing curve segment. As you drag the second direction point, notice that it no longer has any effect on the incoming direction point.

3 Move your cursor to a new position, then continue drawing either smooth or corner points.

Showing and Selecting Paths/Points

Use the following techniques for selecting, deselecting and deleting paths.

1. To select a path, first you have to show it. To do this, click the path entry in the Paths palette. The path now shows in the image window.

2. To select the path, select the Direct Selection tool (the white arrow). Click on the path to make it active. You now see the curve and line segments together with the anchor points that form the path.

3. Click on the anchor point of a curve segment to select the point and display the direction points.

4. To select and move an entire path, show the path, then hold down Alt/option and click on the path. Using the Direct Selection tool, position your cursor on an anchor point or curve segment, then click and drag to reposition the path. To deselect a path, click away from the path using the Direct Selection tool. The path still shows, but is not selected.

5. To delete a path, with a point or line segment of the path selected press Delete twice. Alternatively, with the entire path selected, press Delete once. You can also drag the path name onto the Wastebasket icon in the Paths palette.

Add, Delete and Convert Points

To achieve a precise path, you often need to add points and delete points on a path.

1 To add a point, make sure the path is selected, select the Add Anchor Point tool from the Pen Tool group, position your cursor on the path and then click. If you click on a curve or straight line segment you automatically get an anchor point with direction points.

2 To delete a point, make sure the path is selected, select the Delete Anchor Point tool, position your cursor on an existing anchor point then click. The path redraws without the point.

3 To convert a smooth point into a corner point, select an anchor point with the Direct Selection tool. Select the Convert Point tool, position your cursor on a direction point then click and drag. Use the Direct Selection tool to make any further changes to the direction points.

4 To convert anchor points on straight line segments into smooth points, select the Convert Point tool, position your cursor on the anchor point then click and drag. Direction lines appear around the point. Use the Direct Selection tool to make any further changes to the points.

5 To convert a smooth point into a corner point without direction lines, select the Convert Point tool then click on an anchor point.

Editing Points

Paths invariably need to be modified and fine-tuned to produce the result you require.

1 To edit a smooth point, make sure the path is selected, then click on the anchor point to select it. Direction points appear either side of the anchor point. Direction points control the shape and length of a curve segment.

2 When you drag a direction point of a smooth anchor point, as you change the angle of one side, the other direction point moves to balance the point you are moving. This ensures the curve is always smooth through the anchor point.

3 The further away from the anchor point you drag a direction point, the longer the associated curve segment becomes.

As the curve segment is anchored at the anchor points at either end, this causes the curve segment to bow out more. Bring the direction point closer to the anchor point and the curve segment becomes shorter.

4 When you drag direction points on a corner anchor point, each moves totally independently of the other, allowing a sharp change of direction at the point.

Exporting Paths

Exporting Clipping Paths

Create a clipping path when you want to create transparent areas in an image you intend to use in an application such as QuarkXPress or Adobe InDesign. A clipping path makes areas of the image outside the path transparent, allowing you to see past the outline of the image to the background on which the image is placed.

Flatness allows a PostScript printer to create less memory-intensive paths at output. If you use too high a flatness value, you get an approximate path that does not accurately conform to the path you created. For high-resolution printing (1200-2400 dpi) a flatness value of 8 to 10 should be acceptable. Use a value of 1 to 3 for low resolution printing (300-600 dpi). Leave the field blank to use the printer's default setting. This usually produces good results with most images.

1 Create a saved path (see page 141). If you have more than one path in the Paths palette, make sure you select the appropriate path. Use the Paths palette menu to select Clipping Path.

2 Use the Path pop-up to specify a different path to make into a clipping path if necessary. Enter a Flatness value.

3 When you have saved a clipping path, you need to save the file in EPS or TIFF file format for output. Choose File>Save As. In the Save As dialog box, give the file a name and specify where you want to save it.

Remember to convert the file to an appropriate mode – e.g. CMYK – before you save the file in EPS format.

4 Choose Photoshop EPS or TIFF from the Format pop-up. Click Save. Clipping Paths saved with the image are automatically exported with the file when you save in Photoshop EPS or TIFF file format.

Select a TIFF preview option if you intend to use the image on the Windows platform.

5 See the section on saving in Photoshop EPS format (page 44) for information on Preview and Encoding options.

Save a file with a clipping path in Photoshop EPS format if you are printing the file to a PostScript output device.

6 When you import the file into a QuarkXPress or Adobe InDesign page, the clipping path hides areas of the image outside the clipping path. The second version of the leaf image on this Quark page has a black background and does not have a clipping path.

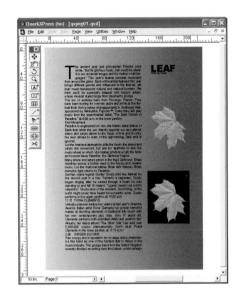

Exporting paths to Adobe Illustrator

Sometimes it is useful to export a path from Photoshop into Adobe Illustrator to perform further manipulation on it.

When you open exported paths in Adobe Illustrator, the crop marks indicate the dimensions of the original Photoshop image.

1 To export a path to Adobe Illustrator, choose File>Export>Paths to Illustrator. In the Export Paths dialog box, change the name if necessary but leave the automatically generated .ai extension to distinguish the file. If your Photoshop document has more than one saved path, use the Paths pop-up to choose the path you want to export. Click Save.

2 Use File>Open in Adobe Illustrator to import the path. Manipulate and make changes to the path as required, then save the Illustrator file in EPS format.

You can use the Export Paths to Illustrator command and then open the file in Macromedia FreeHand if you do not have Adobe Illustrator.

3 See pages 36–37 for information on placing an Illustrator EPS into Photoshop.

Creating Shape Layers

The Shape tools allow you to create lines, rectangles, ovals and circles. In Photoshop you can also create polygons and custom shapes. Use the Options bar to set specific options for each tool individually.

1 To draw a rectangle as a Shape layer, first choose a foreground color for the shape. Select the Rectangle tool. Make sure the Shape Layer button is selected in the Options bar.

2 Position your cursor in the image window. Drag diagonally to define the size of the shape. A new Shape layer appears in the Layers palette. To create additional shapes on the same Shape layer, either choose a new shape tool from the Options bar or use the same tool. Select the Add to Shape Area button in the Options bar. Draw the shape.

3 To draw a square, hold down Shift then drag with the Rectangle tool. Release the mouse button before you release Shift, otherwise the constraint effect will be lost. Hold down Alt/option then drag with the Rectangle tool to draw a rectangle from the center out.

4 Select the Shape layer icon (a highlight border appears around the Shape layer icon), then use the Direct Selection tool to select and then make changes to the shape of the object in the image window.

Channels and Masks

The Channels palette stores color information about an image and can also be used to store selections on a permanent basis.

Masks are created and used in a variety of ways in Photoshop. The basic principle of masks is that you use them to protect areas of an image from editing that you carry out on the unmasked areas of the image.

Use Quick Mask mode when you don't want to save the mask for future use. Layer masks control how different areas of pixels on a layer are hidden or revealed.

Covers

Chapter Eleven

Quick Mask Mode

You can make a rough selection first, then go into Quick Mask mode and edit the mask further if necessary.

In Quick Mask mode you create a 50% red, semi-transparent overlay. This overlay represents the protected area of the image. The overlay is similar in concept to a traditional rubylith mask. Quick Mask mode is particularly useful because you can see both the image and the mask as you create and fine-tune the mask.

1 To create a quick mask, click the Quick Mask Mode icon in the Toolbox. Make sure that the default foreground and background colors are black and white respectively.

2 Show the Brushes palette and choose a brush size. Use a hard-edged brush to create selections with a clearly defined edge. Use a soft-edged brush to create selections that are slightly softer along the edge. Select a painting tool and drag across your image to "paint" in the mask. Painting with black adds to the mask. Although you see through the 50% red mask, the pixels covered by the mask are completely protected.

Painting with gray or any other color creates a semi-transparent or partial mask.

3 To remove areas from the mask you can use the Eraser tool, or paint with white.

4 When you are satisfied with your mask, click the Standard Mode button. This turns the areas of the image that were not part of your quick mask into a selection. You can now make changes to the selected areas (in this example the Box Blur filter has been applied), leaving the areas that were the quick mask unchanged.

The Channels Palette

You can change the display of channels from grayscale to the color they represent by choosing Edit>Preferences>Display and Cursor (Windows), or, Photoshop> Preferences>Display and Cursor (Mac). Select the Color Channels in Color checkbox:

The Channels palette (Window>Channels) shows a breakdown of the color components that combine to make up the composite color image that you work with most of the time on-screen.

For example, in RGB mode, there are four channels – the composite image (all the other channels combined), and then a channel each for the red, green and blue color components of the image. In CMYK mode, there are five channels.

Using the Channels palette you can be selective about which of the color components in your image you change.

1. To switch to a specific channel, click the channel name in the Channels palette. The channel highlights to indicate that it is selected. The image window changes according to the channel you chose.

Indexed Color mode, Grayscale mode and Bitmap mode all have only one channel.

2. You can view additional channels by clicking the Eye icon for a channel. The image window changes, but your editing remains limited to the selected channel.

3. Click on the composite channel to return to normal image-editing view.

Saving and Loading Selections

Because you can only have one "active" selection in an image at any one time, the facility to store a selection which can be reloaded later is vital, especially if the selection is complex and took some time to create. You save selections as an extra channel in the Channels palette. These extra channels are referred to as "alpha channels".

Saving selections

To save a selection to a channel, make your selection on the image, then choose Select>Save Selection. The Save Selection dialog box appears. Specify in which document you wish to save the channel. (You can save channels in another document to keep the file size of the current document as small as possible.)

Leave the Channel pop-up on New. Enter a name for the channel. Click OK. Alternatively, make your selection and then click the Save Selection icon in the Channels palette.

2 An additional channel appears in the Channels palette. This is the new "alpha channel". An alpha channel is a grayscale channel.

3 When you have saved a selection to an alpha channel you can freely deselect the selection in your image, as you can now reselect exactly the same area at any time using the alpha channel.

Loading selections

Use the following process to reselect an area using the alpha channel:

1. To load a channel selection as a selection on the image, make sure the composite image is displayed. You can do this by clicking on the topmost channel name in the Channels palette. Then choose Select>Load Selection. The Load Selection dialog box appears.

2. Use the Channel pop-up menu to specify which channel you want to load. Select an operation as appropriate. The operations allow you to control how the selection you are about to load interacts with any existing selection in the image – adding to it, subtracting from it or intersecting with it. Click OK.

3. Alternatively, using the Channels palette, drag the channel you want to load onto the Load Selection icon.

4. To delete a channel, drag the channel name onto the Wastebasket icon at the bottom of the palette.

Editing Alpha Channel Masks

You can display an alpha channel without loading it onto the image as a selection. You can then edit the mask by painting with black, white or gray.

1 To display an alpha channel, choose Windows>Channels to display the Channels palette. Click on the alpha channel you want to display. The channel name highlight, and an Eye icon in the left column of the palette, indicate that this is the visible channel.

2 The image window changes from the composite view to a grayscale representation of the mask. The white area represents the selection and the black portions represent the protected areas.

3 To edit a selection channel, select a painting tool and brush size. Click the Default Colors icon if necessary, to change the foreground color to black. Paint with black to remove areas from the selection. Paint with white on any black portion of the mask to add it to the selection.

Another useful technique for editing a selection mask is to view a mask and image simultaneously by turning the alpha channel selection into a colored mask (very much like using Quick Mask mode) and then reshaping the mask by painting with black, white or shades of gray.

Typically, when you edit masks, you paint with black or white, with the Mode set to Normal and an Opacity of 100%. However, you can reduce the opacity or pressure settings in order to create a partial mask.

Reshaping masks

1 To reshape a mask, ensure you don't have an active selection on your image. Click on the alpha channel in the Channels palette to select it. It highlights and the Eye icon shows on the left. The image window now displays the grayscale selection channel mask. The Eye icon disappears from the Composite RGB channel and from the individual Red, Green and Blue channels.

Make sure that the Eye icon for an alpha channel mask is not selected, then click the Composite channel when you want to return to the standard editing view.

2 Click in the currently empty Eye icon position for the Composite channel. The eye appears for the Composite channel and in the individual Red, Green and Blue ones. The Composite channel now also shows in the image window but only the alpha channel is selected – indicated by the highlight.

3 The image window changes in appearance. The selection area appears as normal whilst the protected or masked portions of the image have a quick mask type transparent film applied.

4 Select the Brush or Pencil tool. Paint with white to remove areas of the image from the mask (to enlarge the unmasked area). Paint with black to add portions of the image to the mask.

Layer Masks

Use layer masks to hide or reveal areas of a layer. A layer mask is extremely useful because you can use it to try out effects without actually changing the pixels on the layer. When you have achieved the result you want, you can apply the mask as a permanent change. If you are not satisfied, you can discard the mask without having permanently affected the pixels on the layer.

For information on creating layers, see Chapter Eight. For information on using filters, see Chapter Thirteen.

This example begins with an image with two layers. The Background layer is the original scan; the other layer was created using the Render>Clouds filter.

1 To create a layer mask for the Clouds layer, first click on the layer to make it active. Choose Layer>Add Layer Mask>Reveal All. Reveal All makes all the pixels on the layer visible. The Clouds layer now completely obscures the Background layer.

You can have only one layer mask per layer.

2 In the Layers palette, the layer mask is active, indicated by the highlight border on the mask thumbnail. Click on the layer thumbnail to make the layer active. Click on the Layer Mask thumbnail to continue editing the mask.

3 With the layer mask thumbnail selected, make sure that the foreground color is set to black. Choose a Painting tool and start painting. Painting with black hides pixels on the Clouds layer, revealing pixels on the Background layer.

You can paint
with shades of
gray to partially
hide pixels on the
Clouds layer.

4 Pixels on the
Clouds layer are not
permanently erased
when you paint with
black. Paint with white
to show pixels on the
Clouds layer – in effect
hiding pixels on the

Background layer. (If you choose Layer>Add Layer Mask>Hide All,
you start with the opposite scenario to the above. Now all the
pixels on the Clouds layer are hidden. Paint with white to reveal
pixels on the Clouds layer, paint with black to hide them.)

5 To temporarily switch off the layer mask, choose Layer>Layer
Mask>Disable, or hold down Shift then click on the Layer Mask
icon. To reactivate the mask, choose
Layer>Layer Mask>Enable, or hold
down Shift then click again on the
Layer Mask icon.

6 To apply the layer mask as a permanent
change, choose Layer>Layer Mask>Apply. .

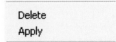

7 To discard the layer mask, without affecting
pixels on the layer, choose Layer>Layer
Mask>Delete. Or, drag the Layer Mask icon
(not the Layer icon) onto the
Wastebasket icon in the bottom
of the palette. Click Apply or
Delete. Once you apply a layer

mask you lose the flexibility of making further changes – the effect
is fixed. Click Delete only if you want to discard the mask.

Channel and Quick Mask Options

The Channel Options dialog box and the Quick Mask Options dialog box allow you to control the color of a mask and whether the protected or unprotected area of the image is colored with the overlay.

1   To change channel options, double-click the alpha channel entry. Alternatively, with the alpha channel selected, use the Channels palette menu to choose Channel Options.

2   In the Channel Options dialog box you can enter a new name for the channel. You can also choose Selected Areas to reverse the way in which the color will apply. In other words, masked (protected) areas will appear white, while the selection area (unprotected) will appear black.

3   To change the color used to represent the masked (protected) area and its opacity, click the Color box and choose a new color from the Color Picker.

4   To change the settings for a quick mask, double-click either the Quick Mask Mode icon or the Standard Mode icon, then make the appropriate changes in the dialog box that appears.

Color Correction Techniques

Color correction involves making changes to the overall brightness and contrast in an image and also the color balance to compensate for any tonal deficiencies and color casts in the original image.

You should bear in mind that although color corrections can improve the overall appearance of an image, inevitably some color values may be lost – certain pixels in the original scan or photograph that were different colors can end up remapped to the same color. The successful use of the commands covered in this chapter can also depend on the accuracy of the colors you see on your monitor.

Covers

Chapter Twelve

Brightness/Contrast and Color Balance

The Brightness/Contrast command provides the least complicated controls for changing overall brightness/contrast levels in an image. It does not change individual color channels; it makes the same adjustment to all pixels across the full tonal range of the image.

To change brightness and contrast for an entire image, or for a selection, choose Image>Adjustments> Brightness/Contrast. Drag the Brightness and Contrast sliders or enter a value in the entry boxes. OK the dialog box.

Choose Image>Adjustments>Auto Contrast to automatically adjust the contrast for an image or selection. Auto Contrast does not adjust individual channels in an image. It makes highlights appear lighter and shadows darker by mapping the lightest and darkest pixels in the image to white and black respectively.

Color Balance works on the principle of complementary colors. If there is too much cyan in an image, you drag the Cyan–Red slider towards red to remove the cyan color cast; for too much magenta, drag the Magenta–Green slider towards green etc.

To adjust the Color Balance of an image, choose Image> Adjustments>Color Balance. Click the Shadows, Midtones or Highlights radio button to specify the tonal range to which you want to make changes. Drag the color sliders to reduce/increase the amount of a color in the image. Select Preserve Luminosity to prevent brightness values from changing as you change color levels. This helps maintain the overall color balance in the image.

Auto Levels and Auto Color

You can also use the Auto Levels command from within the Levels and Curves dialog boxes. Click the Auto button:

Auto Levels allows you to adjust brightness and contrast automatically. Auto Levels examines each color channel independently and changes the darkest pixels to black and the lightest pixels to white, then redistributes the remaining shades of gray between these two points.

Auto Levels works best on images that have a reasonably even distribution of tonal values throughout the image, as it redistributes pixels based on white and black points, with a tendency to increase contrast.

Auto Color removes unwanted color casts in an image without adjusting the contrast in an image.

1 To apply Auto Levels to an image, choose Image>Adjustments> Auto Levels. (Use Edit>Undo if the result is not satisfactory.)

Auto Levels adjusts each color channel in the image individually. As a result, it may remove or sometimes introduce color casts.

2 To apply Auto Color to an image, choose Image>Adjustments> Auto Color. (Use Edit>Undo if the result is not satisfactory.)

Original   Auto Levels   Auto Color

Both Auto Levels and Auto Color generally produce good results, but they do not allow the precision of the manual adjustments that you can make using the Levels and Curves dialog boxes.

The Levels Dialog Box

Use the Levels dialog box (Image>Adjustments>Levels) to adjust the tonal balance for color and grayscale images. You can adjust highlight, shadow and midtone ranges for a selection or an entire image, or you can make changes to individual channels only.

The most flexible way of working with Levels, Curves and Color Balance is to set up Adjustment layers (see page 114). Adjustment layers allow you to repeatedly adjust settings in the respective dialog boxes until you are satisfied with the result.

Input Levels

The Input Levels sliders and entry boxes allow you to improve the contrast in a "flat" image.

1   Use the Channel pop-up menu to select a channel. If you do not select an individual channel, you can work on the composite image and affect all channels.

2   To darken an image, drag the solid black slider to the right. Alternatively, enter an appropriate value in the leftmost Input Levels entry box. This maps or clips pixels to black. For example, if you drag the black slider to 15, all pixels with an original value between 0 and 15 become black. The result is a darker image.

The spiky graph in the middle of the Levels dialog box is a Histogram. See pages 166–167 for an explanation of the Histogram in the Levels dialog box.

Dragging either or both the black or white Input Levels sliders inwards has the effect of increasing contrast in the image.

3   To lighten an image, drag the hollow, white Input Levels slider to the left. Alternatively, enter an appropriate value in the rightmost Input Levels entry box. The result is to map or clip pixels to white. For example, if you drag the white slider to 245, all pixels with an original value between 245 and 255 become white. The result is a lighter image.

Gamma

When you OK the Levels dialog box, you can use Edit>Undo/Redo a number of times to evaluate the changes.

The gray triangle and the middle Input Levels entry box control the Gamma value in the image. The Gamma value is the brightness level of mid-gray pixels in the image.

1 To lighten midtones, drag the gray slider to the left, or increase the Gamma value in the Input Levels entry box above the default setting of 1.00.

2 To darken midtones, drag the gray slider to the right, or decrease the Gamma value in the Input Levels entry box.

See page 161 for an explanation of Auto Levels and the Auto button.

Output Levels

You can use the Output Levels entry boxes or sliders to decrease the amount of contrast in an image.

1 Drag the black Output Levels slider to the right to lighten the image and reduce the contrast.

2 Drag the white Output Levels slider to the left to darken the image and reduce the contrast.

The Curves Dialog Box

The Curves dialog box (Image> Adjustments>Curves) offers the most versatile set of controls for making tonal adjustments in an image. The central Brightness graph in the dialog box displays the original and adjusted brightness values for pixels in the image. The graph is a straight line from 0 (black) to 255 (white), before any adjustments are made – input and output values for pixels are the same.

You should be careful not to click on the Brightness bar at the bottom of the Curves dialog box accidentally.

The default Brightness bar starts black and graduates to white. In this state, the brightness curve indicates the brightness values of colors in the image; the brightness curve starts at 0, for black, and moves to 255, for white.

The horizontal axis of the graph represents the original or input values, the vertical axis represents the output or adjusted values. By adjusting the brightness curve, you are remapping the brightness values of pixels in the image.

1 To add a point to the curve, select the Point tool. Click on the curve. (You can add up to fifteen points.) Drag the point(s) around to edit the curve. Or click at a point in the graph and the curve will change according to where you clicked.

2 To delete a point, click on a point to select it, then press the Delete/Backspace key. You can also drag it outside the Brightness graph.

Select a point on the graph, then press the arrow keys on your keyboard to move the point in increments.

3 To lighten an image, select the Point tool, position your cursor near the midpoint of the graph, then click to place a new point. Click and drag this point upwards.

Hold down Alt/ option, then click on the Reset button (previously Cancel) to restore the original settings in the dialog box.

Click the Expand button ( ) to increase the size of the Curves dialog box.

Hold down Alt/ option then click in the brightness graph to display a finer grid. This can provide greater precision when positioning and manipulating points on the curve.

4 To darken an image, select the Point tool, position your cursor near the midpoint of the graph, then click to place a point. Drag the point downwards.

5 To increase the contrast in an image, place a point at roughly the ¼ tone part of the graph and drag this upwards to lighten the highlights. Next, place a point at roughly the ¾ tone part of the graph. Drag this downward to darken the shadow areas. The result is to increase the contrast in the image by lightening the highlights and darkening the shadows, whilst leaving the midtones more or less untouched.

6 Reverse the setting in step 5 to decrease the contrast in an image.

7 To limit changes to the midtones and highlights, click on the graph to place a point at the ¾ tone. Place a point at the ¼ tone and drag this upwards. Reverse this procedure to change midtones and shadows without affecting highlights.

The Histogram Palette

A histogram is a bar chart that represents the distribution of pixels in an image. Shadows are on the left side of the histogram, highlights on the right and midtones in the middle. The spread of pixels through the shadows, midtones and highlights represents the tonal balance in an image.

In a histogram, the horizontal axis plots color or luminosity levels from 0-255. The vertical axis plots the number of pixels at each level.

Having the Histogram palette visible as you work on an image can help you evaluate the effect of the changes and adjustments you make.

1 The Histogram palette is grouped initially with the Navigator and Info palettes. Click the Histogram tab, or choose Window>Histogram to show the palette.

2 Choose Expand View from the Histogram palette menu to enable access to the Channel drop down menu. Choose from RGB, Luminosity, and Colors to view the histogram for the channel you specify. For an image with more than one layer you can choose Selected Layer from the Source drop down menu to view a histogram for the pixel content on the currently active layer.

Choose Show Channels in Color from the palette menu to display colored histograms for the Red, Green and Blue channels.

3 Choose All Channels View to display an extended palette with histograms for all channels in the image, with the exception of Alpha channels, Spot channels and masks. The topmost histogram represents the luminance, or overall brightness values for the composite channel.

4 For RGB and CMYK images you can choose Colors from the Channel drop down menu to display a composite histogram of the individual color channels in color.

5 To show statistical information for the histogram, choose Show Statistics from the Histogram palette menu. Move your cursor through the bars of the histogram itself to get readouts for Level, Count and Percentile in the statistics area.

6 When working in dialog boxes such as Levels and Curves, provided that the Preview option is selected, the Histogram palette updates as you make changes to the settings in the dialog box.

7 The Cached Data warning icon appears when the Histogram palette display is based on information held in cache (an area of short term memory) rather than the actual current state of the image. To ensure that the histogram represents all pixels in the image in their current state, either click the Cached Data warning icon, or click the Uncached Refresh button. You can also double-click anywhere within the histogram. Photoshop uses cached information for the image in order to display information in the histogram quickly, but slightly less accurately, as the cached information is based on a representative sampling of pixels in the image only.

Shadow/Highlight Command

The Shadow/Highlight command is useful for images with strong backlighting resulting in a silhouette effect on the foreground elements. The default settings in the Shadow/Highlight dialog box are intended to improve images with backlighting problems. You can also use the Shadow/Highlight command to lighten shadows.

Make sure the Preview option is selected to evaluate how changes you make to settings in the dialog box affect the image.

1 To adjust shadows and highlights in an image, choose Image>Adjustments>Shadow/Highlight.

2 Drag the Shadows Amount slider to the right, or enter a value in the percentage entry field from 0–100 to lighten the shadows. The higher the value the greater the degree of lightening.

Choose Image>Adjustments>Photo Filter to access the Photo Filter dialog box. Photo filters simulate traditional photographic lens filters used to warm or cool the overall color content of an image. The Warming (85) and Cooling (80) filters adjust the color temperature of an image. The Warming (81) and Cooling (82) filters are light balancing filters and have less impact on an image.

Use the Density slider to control the strength of the filter effect.

3 Drag the Highlights Amount slider to the right to darken the highlights. You can also enter a value in the percentage entry field. The higher the value the greater the degree of darkening.

Before

After

Match Color Command

Use the Match Color command when you need to make colors in one image (the destination image), consistent with colors in another image (the source image). You can also use this command to match colors between layers within the same image.

The Match Colors command can be useful when you need to match skin tones in one image to the overall color tones in another image.

1. To match colors in an image to colors in a different image, select the destination image. Choose Image> Adjustments>Match Color. If the destination image has multiple layers, make sure you select the layer you want to match before you choose the Match Colors command.

Make sure you have the Preview option selected in order to see how changes you make in the Match Color dialog box affect the destination image.

2. In the Image Statistics area of the dialog box, use the Source drop down menu to select the source image which contains the color characteristics you want to match. If necessary, use the Layer drop down menu to select a specific layer within the source image, or leave the option set to Merged to use the overall color statistics of the source image.

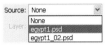

3 In the Image Options area of the dialog box, drag the Fade slider to reduce the intensity of the color adjustment in the target image if necessary. Drag the Luminance slider to increase or decrease the brightness of the result. Drag the Color Intensity slider to increase or decrease the overall color saturation.

Matching colors between layers

1 To match color characteristics from one layer to another in the same image, make sure you have the destination layer (the layer whose color you want to change) selected.

2 Choose Image>Adjustments>Match Color. In the Image Statistics area set the Source drop down menu to the name of the file with which you are working.

3 From the Layer drop down menu select a specific layer, or choose Merged to match color characteristics from the whole of the image.

4 Use the Fade, Luminance and Color Intensity sliders to fine tune the results.

Filters

Photoshop ships with more than 95 filters as standard. Filters add enormous creative flexibility and potential to image-manipulation, and it is well worth spending some time experimenting with them.

You can use filters across an entire image, or you can apply them to selections to limit the results to specific areas. Filters cannot be applied to images in Bitmap or Indexed Color mode. Some filters are not available in CMYK mode.

Covers

Chapter Thirteen

Filter Controls

Use the Filter menu to access the Photoshop filters. Many of the filters have standard controls, which are explained below. Some filters, such as Filters>Stylize>Solarize, do not display a dialog box, but apply the effect immediately. Other filters take you into the Filter Gallery dialog box where you create settings.

1 Click the Preview check box to see the effect of your settings previewed in the main image window, as well as in the Preview window inside the filter dialog box.

2 Click and drag on the image in the Preview window to scroll around to preview different parts of the image. Alternatively, with the filter's dialog box active, position your cursor in the main image window – the cursor becomes a hollow box – then click to set the view in the Preview window.

3 Click the "+" or "-" buttons to zoom in or out on areas of the image. You can also use the Ctrl+Spacebar (Windows) or Command+Spacebar (Mac) keyboard shortcuts within the Preview window or the image window.

4 Hold down Alt/option and click the Reset button (previously Cancel) to revert to the original settings in the dialog box.

5 After you OK a filter's dialog box, use Ctrl+F (Windows) or Command+F (Mac) to reapply the last-used filter and its settings.

Unsharp Mask and Sharpen Filters

These filters allow you to enhance detail in your images.

It is well worth making a copy of your image to work on before you start experimenting with filters.

Unsharp Mask

This is a powerful function which can help you to sharpen blurry images in specific areas. For example, if you rotate an image, or change the dimensions or resolution of the image, it may blur due to any interpolation that Photoshop applies. This can also happen when you convert from RGB to CMYK. Where the Unsharp Mask filter finds edges (areas where there is a high degree of contrast), it increases the contrast between adjacent pixels. The result is to create an apparent improvement in the focus of the image.

To use Unsharp Mask to sharpen an image, choose Filter> Sharpen>Unsharp Mask. The Unsharp Mask dialog box appears.

Set the zoom percentage of the document window to 100% to get an accurate preview of the effect of sharpening in the image. Also, it is preferable to evaluate final results in the actual document window, rather than in the Unsharp Mask preview window.

Adjust settings for Amount, Radius and Threshold. Evaluate changes you make to settings in the Preview window within the dialog box and in the image window itself. Click OK or press Return/Enter.

Amount – Use this to control the amount of sharpening applied to the edges (minimum = 1, maximum = 500). The picture will become pixelated if the amount is too high.

Values below 50% produce subtle results; values between 50% and 250% produce moderate results; while values between 300% and 500% produce dramatic, exaggerated results.

The settings for Radius and Threshold need to be taken into account when setting the Amount value (see the next page).

Radius – Radius controls the depth of pixels along the high-contrast edges that are changed.

A low radius value restricts the impact of the filter; higher values distribute the impact. Radius values of 2.0 or lower usually produce acceptable sharpening.

On high-resolution images, use a Threshold value of 8 or higher to apply the sharpening effect to specific areas only.

Threshold – Sets a level for the minimum amount of contrast between pixels an area must have before it will be modified. The Threshold value is the difference between two adjacent pixels – as measured in brightness levels – that must occur for Photoshop to recognize them as an edge.

High Threshold values limit changes to areas where there is a high degree of color difference. Use low values to apply the filter more generally throughout the image.

Sharpen and Sharpen More

Use the Sharpen and Sharpen More filters when an image becomes blurred after resampling. Both filters work by increasing contrast between adjacent pixels throughout the image or selection. Sharpen More has a more pronounced effect than Sharpen.

Sharpen Edges

This filter has a more specific effect, applying sharpening along high-contrast edges. In effect, it has a less global impact on a selection or image than Sharpen and Sharpen More.

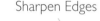

Sharpen Edges   Sharpen More

Sharpen

Unsharp Mask

Smart Sharpen

Sharpening works by increasing contrast where there is already edge detail.

Using too much Sharpening in an image can cause halos and other unwanted artifacts to appear in the image.

The Smart Sharpen filter uses advanced algorithms to produce enhanced sharpening results using an easy to use dialog box with an expanded Preview window, which makes it easier to evaluate the effect of settings on the image.

1 Choose Filter>Sharpen>Smart Sharpen.

2 Set values for Amount and Radius. Amount controls the degree of sharpening. Higher values increase the amount of contrast between neighboring pixels, producing the visual effect of increased sharpness in the image. Radius controls how far the results of sharpening extend into surrounding pixels.

To achieve greater control over sharpening in shadow and highlight areas of an image, select the Advanced radio button. Use the Fade slider in the Highlights and/or Shadows tabs to reduce the overall impact of the sharpening settings specifically in the shadow and highlight tonal ranges.

3 Choose an option from the Remove pop-up menu. Each option uses a different algorithm to sharpen the image. Gaussian

Blur uses the same method as the Unsharp Mask filter. Lens Blur attempts to detect detail where it then increases sharpening, typically producing fewer halos. Use Motion Blur to lessen blur caused by movement of the subject. When you select Motion Blur, set the angle control to specify the direction of the blur.

If you create settings that you want to reuse in the future, you can save the current filter settings. First create the settings you want to save, then click the Save Settings icon ( ) to the right of the Settings pop-up menu:

Enter a name for the settings then click OK. You can now choose the named settings from the Settings pop-up menu.

4 Select the More Accurate checkbox to get the best results, although this can take slightly longer to process.

Blur Filters

The Blur filters reduce the contrast between adjacent pixels along edges where considerable color shifts occur, to create a softening, defocusing effect. Blurring produces the opposite effect to sharpening – which increases the contrast between adjacent pixels.

"Blur" and "Blur More" blur a selection in preset amounts offering only a limited degree of control. For greater control when blurring you can use the Gaussian Blur option, which blurs according to a bell-shaped Gaussian distribution curve.

To Blur a Layer or Selection

Create a selection if you want to limit the effect of the Blur filter to a specific area of your image. Choose Filter>Blur>Blur, or Filter> Blur>Blur More.

Blur More produces an effect roughly 3 times stronger than the Blur filter.

Motion Blur

You can use Motion Blur to create the effect of a moving subject or camera.

To create a motion blur, make a selection, if required. Choose Filter>Blur> Motion Blur.

2 Enter a value in the Angle box, or drag the Angle indicator to specify the angle or direction of the blur. Enter a value in the Distance entry box to specify the distance in pixels for the blur effect. OK the dialog box.

Angle = 0,
Distance = 12

Angle = -45,
Distance = 12

Angle = -53,
Distance = 26

Radial Blur

Radial Blur creates the effect of zooming in as you take a picture.

1 To create a radial blur, make a selection if required. Choose Filter>Blur>Radial Blur.

2 Select a Blur Method and Quality, and specify an Amount (0–100). Click and drag in the Blur Center window to specify the center point for the zoom or spin effect. OK the dialog box.

If you are working on a layer, make sure the Transparency lock is deselected if you want the blur to take effect along the edges of the layer's pixels. (See page 113.)

The Box Blur filter blurs an image or selection using an average color value for neighboring pixels. Increased radius settings create greater blurring. This filter can produce interesting creative effects.

Amount – This value determines the distance pixels are moved to create the blur effect. Higher values produce more intense effects.

Zoom – Zoom creates a zoom-like blurring effect.

Spin – Spin rotates and blurs pixels around a central point.

Quality – Good and Best produce better, smoother results due to the interpolation methods used, but take longer.

Gaussian Blur

Use Gaussian Blur to control the degree of blurring. Gaussian Blur adds low frequency detail to the image or selection. Choose Filter>Blur>Gaussian. Use the Radius slider to adjust the amount of blurring.

Noise Filters

You can use Add Noise to reduce banding in graduated fills.

Add Noise is a good way to begin creating textured backgrounds.

Add Noise filter

The Add Noise filter randomly distributes high-contrast pixels in an image, creating a grainy effect.

To add noise, create a selection, or work on the entire image. Choose Filter>Noise>Add Noise. Specify Amount, Distribution and Monochromatic options.

Amount – Determines the degree to which pixels are changed from their original color. Enter a number from 1–999.

Uniform – Produces an even spread of pixels.

Gaussian – Produces a more dramatic result.

Monochromatic – Choose Monochromatic to distribute grayscale dots.

Original flat background

Amount = 30, Uniform, Monochromatic

Amount = 30, Gaussian, Monochromatic

Dust & Scratches filter

Use the Dust & Scratches filter to remove small imperfections and blemishes in a scan caused by dust and scratches. The degree of success you have with this filter depends largely on the image or selection you apply it to.

To remove dust and scratches, create a selection or work on the entire image. Choose Filters>Noise>Dust & Scratches. Specify Radius and Threshold settings. Click OK.

Radius and Threshold settings are interdependent, and both are taken into account before changes are made.

Radius – Determines how small a blemish must be for it to be worked upon by the filter. For example, at a radius of 3 pixels, the Dust & Scratches filter will not attempt to make changes to imperfections above this size.

Threshold – Specifies the minimum amount of contrast between pixels there must be before changes are made.

Despeckle filter

This produces the opposite effect to the Add Noise filter, smoothing and blurring the image, but having little effect on edges.

Median filter

The Median filter also removes noise from a poor-quality scan. It works by averaging the color of adjacent pixels in an image.

To use the Median filter, create a selection, or work on the entire image. Choose Filter>Noise>Median. Specify a Radius value (1–100). OK the dialog box.

Reduce Noise Filter

Image noise is often apparent in images captured on budget digital cameras and in images saved using high JPEG compression settings. The Reduce Noise filter attempts to remove unwanted noise artifacts whilst retaining edge detail.

1 To remove noise artifacts, choose Filter>Noise>Reduce Noise. Drag the strength slider to increase or decrease the overall impact of the filter on the image. This affects all channels in the image.

2 Create the settings you require to reduce the appearance of noise artifacts. Either drag the sliders to control the settings, or enter a value in the % entry boxes. High Preserve Details settings retain detail along edges and in areas such as hair, but lead to less noise reduction overall in the image. Reduce Color Noise removes random color pixels.

3 Select the Remove JPEG Artifact checkbox to compensate for noise typically found in images saved using high JPEG compression settings.

The Extract Command

There are 4 steps to extracting an object from its background. First, highlight the edges of the object. Second, define the interior of the object. Third, preview the results of the extraction. Four, depending on the preview, fine-tune the extraction, then OK the dialog box.

Use the Extract command to isolate an object from its background; especially useful when the object has edges that are not clearly or distinctly defined, such as hair. Make sure you are working on a layer to use the Extract command. If you perform the Extract command on the Background layer it becomes Layer 0 when you OK the dialog box.

1 To extract an object from its background, choose Image>Extract.

When the object and its background are similar in color or have textures, select the Smart Highlight option. This creates a clearly defined edge highlight, just wide enough to cover the edge, and is not dependent on the brush size.

2 Select the Edge Highlighter tool (B). In the Tool Options area, set a brush size and choose a color for the edge highlight from the Highlight pop-up.

Don't be tempted to rush the process of creating the highlighted edge.

3 Zoom in on the image if necessary, then draw around the object you want to extract to define the edge. It is important to create a highlight that slightly overlaps both the edge of the foreground object and its background. Use a larger brush size to completely cover more delicate, intricate, "wispy" areas of the foreground object, such as hair; use a smaller brush size to highlight sharper, more defined edges.

Use the "[" or "]" keys to decrease/increase the brush size in single increments.

Use Alt/option +Backspace to erase the entire highlight.

4 Use the Eraser tool to undo any mistakes you make with the Edge Highlighter tool. You can use the Undo command within the Extract dialog box to undo the last brush stroke.

To use an alpha channel as the basis for a selection, choose the alpha channel from the Channel pop-up menu.

Use the Zoom and Hand tools as you would in the Photoshop image window. (See page 24 for further information).

When you have filled an interior area with the Fill tool, clicking again in the fill area clears the fill.

Use the Smooth control in the Extraction area, if necessary, to improve the result of the extraction. The Smooth control can help remove stray artifacts from the extraction by feathering edges slightly.

5 Make sure you completely enclose the object if it has a well-defined interior. It is not necessary to highlight edges where the object touches the edge of the image window.

6 Select the Fill tool (G). Click inside the highlight edge. The interior fills with the Fill color set in the Tool Options area of the dialog.

7 Click the Preview button to preview the results. Use the Display pop-up in the Preview area to set the background against which you see the extracted object. It can help to preview against more than one background color to pick up on any problem areas, before you click OK. (See page 183 for techniques to refine the extraction area.)

8 Use the Show pop-up to switch between the original and extracted images. Again, this is useful for making decisions about the results of the extraction before you OK the dialog box.

9 OK the dialog box to complete the extraction.

Fine Tuning Extractions

After you preview the results of the extraction, you will need to fine-tune it, before you OK the dialog box.

1   To make adjustments to the extraction, select the Show Highlight option in the Preview area. The original highlight edge reappears. Choose Original from the View pop-up. The solid background against which you preview the results of the extraction disappears and the original background pixels reappear.

2   Use the Eraser tool to erase parts of the highlight edge and use the Edge Highlighter tool to redefine areas of the edge, as necessary.

3   When you finish editing the highlight edge, select the Fill tool, then click inside the edge to recreate the fill area. Click the Preview button to preview your changes. Repeat the editing process as necessary until you are satisfied with the result.

4   If there are still problems with the extraction, switch off the edge highlight. Use the Clean Up tool to remove any unwanted pixels around the extraction after you preview it. Hold down Alt/option, then drag with the Clean Up tool to refill any unwanted gaps in the extracted object.

5   Use the Edge Touch Up tool to create a more clearly defined, sharper edge in areas where there are problems with the extraction.

6   Click OK to finish the extraction.

The Liquify Dialog Box

The Liquify dialog box allows you to create a wide variety of distortions for retouching images or for achieving creative effects. The dialog box has tools that can push, pull, rotate, reflect, pucker and bloat areas of the image.

Use the Zoom and Hand tools as you would in the standard Photoshop image window.

1   To distort an entire layer, select the layer, or make a selection on a layer to define an area for distortion. Choose Filter>Liquify.

2   Freeze areas of the image that you don't want to change using the Freeze Mask tool. Set a Brush size, then drag across areas of the image you want to freeze. Frozen areas appear as a semi-transparent, red mask. Use the Thaw Mask tool to make frozen areas editable again.

You must rasterize a Type layer or a Shape layer before you can use the Liquify command.

3   Select a tool with which to distort the image, then set tool options. (See the facing page for information on the tools.) Choose a brush size from the Brush Size slider. Set a brush pressure. Lower

Only the active layer is distorted by the liquify dialog box.

pressure settings distort the image more slowly allowing you more control over the distortion. Brush Density controls the softness of the edge of the brush. Choose Turbulent Jitter settings to control how tightly the Turbulence tool distorts pixels.

4   Drag in the image to create the distortion. You can press the left mouse button without dragging the mouse to create effects with tools such as the Twirl tools. Set a Brush Rate to control the speed at which distortions happen when you keep the mouse still. Click OK to accept the changes.

Liquify Distortion Tools

There are 7 distortion tools to choose from. Remember to create tool settings for Brush size, Pressure and Turbulent Jitter before you use the tools. Distortions are most pronounced at the center of the brush area. You can create distortions by dragging across pixels, or simply by holding down the left mouse button.

Use the Reconstruct tool to restore pixels to their original state:

1 Use the Forward Warp tool to distort pixels in a forward direction as you drag.

2 Use the Turbulence tool to smoothly mix or scramble pixels. This can sometimes create interesting cloud and wavelike effects.

3 Use the Twirl Clockwise tool to rotate pixels around the brush area in a clockwise direction. Hold down Alt/option to twirl in a counter clockwise direction.

Hold down Alt/ option then click the Restore all button to revert to the original state of the image.

4 Use the Pucker tool to concentrate pixel detail into the center of the brush area.

5 Use the Bloat tool to disperse image detail away from the center of the brush.

6 Use the Mirror tool to copy pixels into the brush area. The tool reflects the area perpendicular to the direction of the stroke.

7 Use the Push Left tool to move pixels to the left when you drag upward, to the right when you drag downward.

Pattern Maker

Use the Pattern Maker plug-in to generate patterns based on a selected area of an image. You can create and preview multiple pattern variations until you find one you like.

1 Open an image that will provide the sample pixels for the pattern. Choose Filter>Pattern Maker.

You cannot make a pattern from a non-rectangular selection.

Work with a copy of an image when using the Pattern Maker: when you OK the dialog box, the new pattern tiles fill the image window.

2 Use the Selection tool to create a selection to form the basis of the pattern. Click the Generate button to preview the results.

3 Experiment with settings in the Tile Generation area of the dialog box. Then click the Generate Again button. Repeat the process as required.

4 Use the Tile History controls to move backward and forward through the patterns you have generated. OK the dialog box when you have created a pattern you want to utilize.

Filter Gallery

The Filter Gallery allows you to preview and apply individual or multiple filter effects to an entire image, a layer or a selection.

To show the Filter Gallery, choose Filter>Filter Gallery. A preview of the image, with the currently selected filter applied, appears on the left of the window.

Click the Reveal/Hide triangle for each filter category to show or hide the filters available for that category.

Click a filter thumbnail to apply it to the preview. Use the individual controls on the right hand side of the window to experiment and create the settings you want to use. Each filter effect has its own, specific set of controls.

In the Preview area, use the "-" or "+" buttons, or the zoom pop-up to zoom in or out on an area of the preview. Position your cursor in the preview area, then click and drag to reposition the preview.

5 Use the Reveal/Hide button
(⌃) to hide the filter
thumbnails area to create a
larger preview area if necessary.
You can choose filters by name
from the Filter drop down menu
if you hide the thumbnails.

Glass
Glass
Glowing Edges
Grain
Graphic Pen
Halftone Pattern
Ink Outlines
Mosaic Tiles
Neon Glow
Note Paper
Ocean Ripple
Paint Daubs
Palette Knife
Patchwork
Photocopy
Plaster
Plastic Wrap
Poster Edges
Reticulation
Rough Pastels
Smudge Stick
Spatter
Sponge
Sprayed Strokes
Stained Glass
Stamp
Sumi-e
Texturizer
Torn Edges
Underpainting
Water Paper

6 To apply more than one filter to
the preview, click the New Effect
button (⊡) at the bottom
of the window, then click on
another filter effect thumbnail.
The new filter is added to the
bottom of the filter effect list.

7 In the Filter effect
list area, click the
Eye icon box to
apply or hide
the filter effect.
Drag the filter
effect upward or
downward to change the order in which the filters are applied.
Drag a filter effect into the Wastebasket to remove it.

👁	Mosaic Tiles
	Bas Relief
👁	Glass

8 OK the Filter Gallery dialog box when you are ready to apply
the settings.

Vanishing Point

The Vanishing Point filter makes it possible to maintain accurate and correct perspective when you edit an image that contains perspective planes. Use the filter to define a perspective grid, or plane, to establish a vanishing point. You can then make edits within the grid that conform to the correct perspective.

To delete a perspective grid, select the Edit Plane tool, then press the Backspace or Delete button.

I To edit in perspective, choose Filter>Vanishing Point. To define a perspective grid, select the Create Plane tool.

2 Position your cursor on the image, then click to set the first node for the plane. Move you cursor to a new position (do not hold down the mouse button and drag). Click to set the next node. Repeat the process to set a third and fourth corner node. The grid appears in blue in the Vanishing Point window.

Working with the Create Plane tool, use the Show Edges checkbox to control the visibility of the perspective grid. Use the Grid Size pop-up to specify the frequency of the grid.

3 A blue bounding box indicates a valid grid. If the grid or bounding box turns yellow or red as you create or edit it, there is a problem with the alignment of the perspective plane. Typically, the plane doesn't line up correctly with perspective in the image. To correct this, select the Edit Plane tool ( ), position your cursor on a corner node of the perspective grid, then click and drag to adjust the grid to line up with elements in the image.

Using the Create Plane tool, hold down Ctrl/ Command then drag a center top/bottom, or center left/right node to define an additional perpendicular plane.

4   To change the size of the perspective grid rectangle, make sure you drag either the center left/right, or center top/bottom handle.

Removing objects in perspective

1   Create a perspective grid then select the Stamp tool. The grid disappears, to facilitate editing, but the bounding box remains visible. Create settings for the diameter, hardness and opacity of the brush in the Options bar. (See Chapter 5, The Painting Tools, for further information on these controls).

2   Position your cursor over the source pixels – the area you want to use as a sample point. Hold down Alt/option, then click the mouse button to set the sample point, then release the Alt/option key.

3   Reposition you cursor over the target pixels – the area in the image where you want to paint out detail with pixels from around the sample point. Notice as you move your cursor towards the rear of the perspective grid that the cursor size changes to match the grid and maintain the correct perspective.

4   Click and drag to remove unwanted detail. Repeat steps 2–4, if necessary, in order to use slightly different sample points so that the result appears in keeping with the rest of the image and as natural as possible.

Web and Multimedia Images

The success of the World Wide Web is in no small part due to its ability to include images in HTML pages. This section looks at some of the considerations for using different image types effectively in formats suited to the environment of the WWW. It also covers techniques for using images in multimedia work.

Balancing file size and image quality is a primary concern when creating images for Web and multimedia use. Generally, the smaller the file size, the quicker the image will load and display on screen. The following techniques examine ways of reducing file size without losing too much image quality.

An image resolution of 72 ppi is usually satisfactory for images intended for screen-based presentations.

Covers

Chapter Fourteen

Save for Web

The Save for Web command offers comprehensive controls for saving images to be used on the World Wide Web. Use the Save for Web command when you want to create an image that is as small as possible – to ensure the fastest possible download times – without sacrificing too much quality.

1 Choose File>Save to save any changes you have made to the image in the current file format. Then choose File>Save for Web.

2 In the Save for Web dialog box, click the 2-Up tab to compare the original image and the image with optimization

settings applied. Click the Original tab to view only the original Photoshop image. Click the Optimized tab to view the image with optimization settings applied. When viewing 2-Up and 4-Up, each optimized pane indicates file format, size, and approximate download time for a specific modem speed in the annotations area.

3 In 2-Up or 4-Up view, make sure the Optimized pane is selected – indicated by a blue border. In the Optimize panel, choose an optimization level from the Presets pop-up menu. The Optimized image pane updates so that you can evaluate different options.

...cont'd

The arrangement of the 4-Up panes varies according to the size of the Save for Web dialog box and the dimensions and orientation of the image.

To return an optimized version of the image to its original state, select the Optimized pane, then choose Original from the bottom of the Optimization Presets pop-up menu:

For an image that contains slices, click the Slices Visibility button to view the slices in the Save for Web dialog box:

4 In 4-Up view, choose Repopulate Views from the Optimization pop-up menu to update the remaining panes with lower quality optimization settings.

Optimization: 4-Up View

The 4-Up tab is particularly useful because it allows you to preview images using a variety of optimization levels before you decide which level of optimization you want.

1 Click the 4-Up tab to view the Original image, the image optimized using the current optimization settings set in the Optimization panel, and two lower quality variations of the current optimization settings.

2 To use one of the lower quality comparison panes as the Optimized image, click inside one of the panes to select it. A blue highlight border on the pane indicates that it is selected. Choose Repopulate Views from the Optimization panel pop-up menu. The selected pane becomes the Optimized image. Its optimization settings appear in the Optimization area. The comparison panes update with lower quality optimization settings.

3 To compare different, unrelated optimization settings, click on a comparison pane to select it, then choose an optimization setting from the Settings pop-up. In this case, make sure you do not use the Repopulate Views command.

Preview & Save Optimized Images

You can preview an optimized image in a Web browser before you make a final decision on which optimization settings to use. This can be a useful check before committing yourself to saving the file.

Choose a browser from the Browser Preview pop-up from the bottom of the dialog box. The browser launches and displays the image from the selected pane. Image details such as file format, dimensions and file size are listed below the image. Below the image details is the HTML code necessary to display the image.

To save an optimized image, select the pane with the settings you want to use. Click Save in the Save for Web dialog box.

Use standard Windows/Macintosh techniques to navigate to the folder in which you want to save the image. Enter a file name for the image. The file extension for the optimization settings is automatically appended to the file name. Make sure you don't delete it. The file is saved using the current settings in the Optimize panel.

4   Select HTML and Images from
the Save as Type pop-up
menu, to generate the
code necessary to display
the image in a separate
HTML file. This file is
automatically named
and saved in the same
folder as the optimized

image. The optimized image is saved in an images folder which
Photoshop creates automatically within the folder you specify.

5   To specify whether the HTML file uses a table, or Cascading Style
Sheets to display an image with
slices, choose Other from the
Settings pop-up menu. Choose
Slices from the pop-up menu.
Create the settings you require
in the Slice Output area of the
Output Settings dialog box.

6   For images that contain slices, use the Slices pop-up menu
to choose whether to save all slices in the image, or only the
currently selected slice. Each slice is saved as a separate file and
named according to the settings in the Output Settings dialog box.

7   To change the way in which
slices are named, in the Output
Settings dialog box choose
Saving Files from the pop-up
menu. Use the File Naming
pop-ups to make changes.

GIF Optimization Settings

The GIF file format usually provides the most efficient and flexible optimization controls for images which have areas of flat color, with sharp edges and type, as you often find in logos and buttons.

You cannot use the Lossy option with the Interlaced option, or with a Noise or Pattern dither.

1 To optimize an image using GIF file format, select the image pane for which you want to create the settings. To create a setting for a slice, use the Slice Select tool to select a slice.

2 Choose one of the preset GIF settings from the Preset pop-up menu. Or, to create custom GIF settings, choose GIF from the Format pop-up, then specify settings using the options in the palette.

Avoid using GIF format if your image contains a gradient. Use JPEG format instead (see page 197).

3 Drag the pop-up Lossy slider or enter a value to reduce file size by discarding color information. Values of 5–10 can often be applied without noticeably degrading the image quality. Choose a color palette (see pages 200–201) and a dither method (see page 202).

4 Use the Colors pop-up menu to specify the maximum number of colors in the Color palette. Increase the Web Snap setting to shift colors to their closest Web palette equivalents to help avoid dithering in a browser.

The Interlaced option creates an image that first downloads as a low-resolution preview whilst the full file information is downloaded.

5 Select Transparency to preserve any transparent areas in the image. You can choose a Matte color if you want to blend the edges of transparent areas into the background of a Web page. Use the Transparency pop-up to choose a dither type for the blended areas if required.

JPEG Optimization Settings

JPEG optimization works best on continuous-tone images such as photographs. JPEG compression can preserve more detail in photographic-type images than GIF and still provide considerable file size reduction.

JPEG compression is "lossy". In order to make the file size of an image smaller, some image data is discarded, reducing the quality of the image.

1 To optimize an image using JPEG file format, select the image pane for which you want to create the settings. To create a setting for a slice, use the Slice Select tool to select a slice.

2 Choose one of the preset JPEG settings from the Preset pop-up menu. Or, to create custom JPEG settings, choose JPEG from the format pop-up, then specify settings using options in the palette.

3 Use the Quality pop-up to choose a quality setting, or drag the pop-up Quality slider. Use a high setting to preserve most detail in the image with a larger file size. Reduce the quality setting to achieve greater compression and a smaller file size but with reduced image quality.

For medium to high JPEG compression settings, you can use a small Blur value, e.g. 0.1 to 0.5 to blur pattern artifacts that may appear along sharp edges. Higher values may reduce image detail noticeably.

4 Select the Optimized checkbox to create JPEGs with a slightly smaller file size. Some older browsers do not recognize this setting. Choose Progressive to cause the image to download to the browser in a number of passes, each pass building more detail into the image until it downloads completely. Use Blur settings, if required, to allow greater compression on the file. Settings of less than 0.5 are recommended.

5 JPEG compression does not support transparency in images. You can fill transparent areas with a Matte color to simulate transparency, provided you know the background color against which the image will be viewed.

PNG File Format

PNG is a relatively new file format for saving images for use on the Web. There are 2 PNG file format options: PNG-8 and PNG-24.

As a relatively new image file format, not all browsers, especially older browsers, can display images in PNG format.

PNG-8

PNG-8 file format uses 8-bit color which allows a maximum of 256 colors in an image. It is most effective at compressing areas of solid, flat color, typically found in line art, logos and illustrations with type.

For images which use a very limited range of colors, the GIF format can produce smaller file sizes than PNG-8. Use the 4-Up tab when saving images to choose the best optimization level.

PNG-8 is a lossless compression formula – no color information is lost during compression. Depending on the image, PNG-8 compression can produce files 10–30% smaller than the same image compressed using GIF format.

PNG-8 file format can support background transparency and background matting. Background matting enables you to blend the edges of an image into the background color you set as the background color of your Web page.

PNG-24

Multilevel transparency is not supported by all browsers.

PNG-24 supports 24-bit color which allows millions of colors in the image. Like JPEG, this is a good format when you want to preserve subtle transitions in tone and color in a photographic type image.

PNG-24 uses a lossless compression formula – no color information is discarded during compression. As a result, PNG-24 file sizes are typically larger than if you save the image using JPEG file format.

PNG-24 supports background transparency and background matting. PNG-24 also supports multilevel transparency which allows greater control over the way in which an image blends into the background color of a Web page.

Indexed Color Mode

You can convert RGB or Grayscale images to Indexed Color mode.

Indexed Color mode is an important factor in the preparation of images for use on the World Wide Web and in multimedia applications. It provides an efficient method for reducing the size of a color image. When you work on RGB color images in Photoshop, these are typically 24-bit images, capable of displaying over 16 million colors. Indexed Color Mode converts images to single channel, 8-bit images, capable of displaying a maximum of 256 colors.

Make a selection before you convert to Indexed Color mode, to weight the color table towards the colors that occur in the selection.

1 To convert an RGB color image to Indexed Color mode, choose Image>Mode>Indexed Color.

2 Use the Palette pop-up to specify a color palette which controls and limits the colors that will be used in the image. (See the next page.)

For Uniform, Perceptual, Selective and Adaptive color palettes you can set an exact number of colors to include. Enter a value below 256.

3 Choose an option from the Forced pop-up to force the inclusion of certain colors in the color table.

Local color palettes are based on colors present in the active image. Master color palettes are based on a master color palette created in ImageReady.

4 Select Transparency to preserve any transparent areas in the image. Deselect Transparency to fill transparent areas with the Matte color. White is used if there is no Matte color selected. Matte is only available if there are areas of transparency. (See page 203 for more information.)

5 Set dithering options. (See page 202).

Color Palettes

When working with GIF compression settings you can also choose color palettes from the Palette pop-up in the Optimize area of the Save for Web dialog box in Photoshop and the Optimize Palette in ImageReady.

A color palette controls the 256 possible colors that exist in an Indexed Color or GIF image. Photoshop/ImageReady uses three methods for creating color tables in images: dynamic, fixed and custom.

Dynamic – Perceptual, Selective and Adaptive color palettes are created dynamically. Each time you optimize the image, the palette created is based on the colors occurring in the image. Different images will generate different palettes.

Fixed – the Web, Mac OS, Windows, Black & White and Grayscale color palettes are fixed. There is a limited, or fixed range of colors. If your optimization settings specify fewer than 256 colors, this reduced range of colors is drawn from the fixed color table.

Custom – Custom palettes use colors created or modified by the user. Existing GIF and PNG-8 files also have custom palettes.

System palettes

This is the standard, 8-bit system palette of either the Macintosh or Windows system.

Exact

If the image you are converting already has fewer than 256 colors, Exact is the default. The actual number of colors is indicated in the Colors entry box. You cannot dither an Exact palette.

Web

This is a palette reduced to 216 or fewer colors. Use this palette to achieve consistency across different platforms and when you want to use more than one image on the same Web page. Images which are based on different color palettes can look artificial when seen side by side.

Uniform

This palette is based on a uniform sampling of colors from the color spectrum.

Adaptive

This palette is built around the colors that actually occur in an image. For individual images, it gives better results than Web, as the color table is created by sampling colors from the most frequently occurring areas of the color spectrum in the image.

Custom

This option takes you into the Color Table dialog box and allows you to create your own custom color table.

Previous

Previous is only available after you have converted an image using Adaptive or Custom methods. It uses exactly the same palette as created by the previous conversion.

Perceptual

The Perceptual option creates a color palette biased towards colors to which the human eye is most sensitive.

Selective

This is similar to Perceptual, but biased towards broad areas of color in the image and also the preservation of Web colors. Selective is the default.

Indexed Color Mode converts images to single channel, 8-bit image, capable of displaying a maximum of 256 colors. To convert an RGB color image to Indexed Color mode, choose Image>Mode>Indexed Color.

You can specify an exact number of colors for an Indexed Color image if you don't want the maximum 256 steps. Choose Image>Mode>Indexed Color. Enter a value in the Colors field.

Dithering

Dithering is a technique used to simulate colors that are not actually in the color palette. On computer monitors that support only 256 colors, dithering takes place to simulate a greater range of colors in an image than the monitor is actually capable of displaying. For Web images this is referred to as browser dither. Dithering juxtaposes pixels of different colors to create the illusion of additional colors.

Dithering is not recommended for JPEG images.

You can choose a dithering method for an image when you optimize it. This is referred to as application dither – the dither is built into the image.

To minimize the occurrence of browser dither, create the image using only Web-safe colors.

For GIF images, in the Save for Web dialog box, choose an option from the Dither pop-up. For Diffusion, set a Dither Amount. Higher values result in more dithering which creates the appearance of a greater number of colors in the image. Higher values can also increase the file size, depending on the image.

No Dither
No dithering is applied to the image.

Images with areas of solid color may compress best with Dither set to None. Images with gradients usually need dithering to prevent obvious banding.

Pattern
This creates a square dither pattern, similar to halftones, to simulate colors not available in the color table.

Diffusion
The results of Diffusion are usually less noticeable than Pattern as the dithering is spread across a range of pixels.

Noise
Applies a random dither pattern. This option can be used for images with slices.

Save As JPEG

For a general introduction to the JPEG format, see page 45.

JPEG is a compression format, widely used for preparing images for the World Wide Web. Use JPEG when you are working with photographic-type images, and when preserving color detail and quality in the image are more important than download time considerations. JPEG does not allow transparency, and file sizes may be larger than for images exported in GIF format, depending on the compression level you choose.

To save an image in JPEG format, choose File>Save As. Specify a location, enter a name, then choose JPEG from the Formats pop-up. OK the dialog box.

Save images with gradients in the JPEG format, as this format typically produces smaller file sizes than GIFs with an Adaptive palette.

Choose a color from the Matte pop-up to simulate background transparency in the image. You need to know the background color of the Web page, in order to match the matte color to it.

JPEG is most suited to compressing continuous-tone images (images in which the distinction between immediately neighboring pixels is slight). JPEG is not the best format for saving flat color images.

Use the Quality pop-up to specify the amount of compression, or drag the slider. "Maximum" gives best quality, retaining most of the detail in the image, but least compression. "Low" gives lowest image quality, but maximum compression.

For Format Options, choose Baseline Optimized to optimize the color quality of the image. Select Progressive and enter a number for Scans to download the image in a series of passes which add detail progressively until the image is completely displayed. Click OK to export the file.

Web Photo Gallery

The Web Photo Gallery command allows you to set up a website that features your images, quickly and simply, without the need to write any HTML. The website has a home page with thumbnail image links to other pages with full-size images, and includes navigation buttons.

1   To create a Web Photo Gallery choose File>Automate>Web Photo Gallery.

2   Choose a template to control the look and feel of the website from the Styles pop-up menu. A thumbnail of the style appears on the right of the dialog box. Include an e-mail address if you want viewers to be able to contact you via e-mail.

3   In the Options area, use the pop-up menu to specify settings for text labels on the site, and to specify size and compression settings for thumbnail and full-size images.

4   Click the Browse button to navigate to the folder which contains the images you want to include on the website. Click the Destination button to navigate to the folder in which you want Photoshop to create the website. Click OK, then test the Web Photo Gallery in a browser.

Working with ImageReady

With the rapid, commercial development of the World Wide Web since the mid 1990's onward, there has been a growing need for a distinct set of controls and features that allow the user to create eye-catching, optimized images with small file sizes for rapid download times on modems. Creating images for the Web brings a different range of possibilities, technical requirements and constraints when compared with creating images destined to be printed on paper.

ImageReady is designed specifically to meet these rapidly emerging needs. It has dedicated optimization controls and you can create animated GIF files, slices, rollovers and image maps.

Covers

Chapter Fifteen

Photoshop and ImageReady

You can work on an image in Photoshop, then continue to make further adjustments to the same image in ImageReady, or vice versa. Use the Edit in ImageReady/ Photoshop button or command to move images seamlessly from one environment to the other so that you can work in the environment that gives you the most control for whatever task you are attempting.

ImageReady and Photoshop exist as separate application environments, yet work side by side with one another. Much of the toolset and many of the palettes and working techniques are identical in both environments. ImageReady is specifically optimized for creating images for the Web and multimedia, whereas Photoshop provides a powerful feature set for creating images for print, but at the same time provides controls for the creation of images destined for the screen.

Moving between applications

1 For an image you've begun to prepare in Photoshop, choose File>Edit in Image Ready. Or click the Edit in ImageReady button.

2 ImageReady then launches and the image appears in the ImageReady application window. You can now make further changes to the image in ImageReady. The image moves from the Photoshop application environment to the ImageReady environment.

Many of the ImageReady palettes have the same range of functionality as their counterparts in Photoshop. The Web Content, Animation, Slice, Image map and Rollover palettes are available in ImageReady only.

Individual or multiple changes you make in one application environment are represented in the History palette of the other application as a single entry called "Update from File".

3 To move the image currently active in ImageReady back into the Photoshop working environment again, click the Edit in Photoshop button, or choose File>Edit in Photoshop.

The ImageReady Toolbox & Window

The ImageReady Toolbox is largely the same as the Photoshop Toolbox. This page indicates the tools found in ImageReady which are not found in Photoshop, and indicates how to create Tear-off tool groups.

Image Map tools

Button tools

Some tools, such as the Paint Bucket and Clone Stamp tool, are found in different locations in the ImageReady toolbox.

1 To create a Tear-off tool palette, position your cursor on a tool group (indicated by the small triangle). Press and hold the mouse button, move it onto the Tear-off bar at the bottom of the palette and then release the mouse button.

Hide/Show Slices

Hide/Show Image Maps

Preview Document

Preview in Browser

2 Use the Status Bar Display pop-ups to choose readouts that help you make decisions about the image on which you are working.

Optimize tabs

Status Bar display pop-up

Creating and Saving Images

In ImageReady's New Document dialog box there is no Color Mode pop-up. Images in ImageReady are always in RGB mode.

Although creating and saving images in ImageReady is very similar to the same routines in Photoshop, there are some differences to be aware of.

1 To create a new file in ImageReady, choose File>New. Enter values in pixels for Width and Height, or use the Size pop-up to choose a preset size. There is no need to give the file a name at this stage.

In the ImageReady New Document dialog box you do not set a resolution. The resolution of images in ImageReady is always 72 ppi.

2 Choose an option from the Contents of First Layer area. Select White to fill the default layer with White. Choose Background to fill the layer with the current Background color. Choose Transparent to create a transparent layer.

You work in Photoshop file format (.PSD) as you build and edit an image. Optimize the image when you have finished working on it and want to prepare it for the WWW.

3 To save a file in the first instance, choose File>Save As. In the Save dialog box, specify a location in which you want to save the file. Enter a name. The .PSD file extension is automatically added to the file name. Make sure you retain the file extension. Click the Save button. Continue to work on the file in Photoshop format and use the Save command (Ctrl/Command+S) regularly to save changes you make.

| File name: | Untitled-1.psd |
| Save as type: | Photoshop (*.psd) |

Make sure you are working in the Original tab to edit and change the image.

4 When the image is finished and you want to save an optimized version for use on the World Wide Web or in a multimedia application, use the Save Optimized As command. (See page 214 for information on saving optimized files.)

Handling Type in ImageReady

With the Type tool selected, click and drag in the image window to create Paragraph type. (See page 131 for further information.)

Type is entered and edited directly in the image window, as it is in Photoshop.

1 To enter type, choose the Type tool, position your cursor in the image window, then click to place the text insertion point.

2 Enter type using the keyboard. The type automatically creates a new Type layer in the Layers palette. The new layer is positioned above the previously active layer. Type appears formatted with the current settings in the Type palettes. Select a different layer, or choose a different tool, to continue working with the image.

With the Type tool selected, click the Change Text Orientation button in the Options bar to create vertical type:

3 To make changes to the formatting of type, select the Type tool. Position your cursor carefully on the text or you may find that you create a new type layer accidentally. Drag across the text in the image window. You can highlight type in this way, even if the Type layer is not active. Alternatively, just click on a type layer to make it active if you want to change the formatting for the entire layer.

You should consider using slightly larger type when working with images for the Web than you would for printed images.

4 To change type settings, with the Type tool selected, choose options from the Options bar.

...cont'd

When choosing an anti-aliasing level for type, make sure you are viewing the image at actual size to get the best feel for how the type will appear when viewed by the end user.

In ImageReady, pixels are the only unit of measurement for type.

Choose View> Show>Smart Guides to switch off smart alignment guides if you find them distracting. Use the same option to switch them back on again.

5 Click the Palettes button in the Options bar to display the Character and Paragraph palettes. These palettes offer the full range of controls available in Photoshop and ImageReady. (See pages 133–135 for information on using the Character and Paragraph palettes.)

6 When a Type layer is active and when you choose any tool other than the Type tool, the type highlights with a blue line running across the base of the type and a small square indicates the current alignment setting for the type.

7 To reposition type, make sure the Type layer is active, select the Move tool (   ), then drag the type. As you reposition a type layer, or any other layer in ImageReady, alignment guides appear as you drag. Use these interactive alignment guides to align the contents of layers accurately.

8 With a type layer selected, select the Show Transform Box to display a transformation bounding box around the type. Drag a handle to transform the type visually. (See page 120 for further information on transforming layers.)

The Shape Tools

Use the Rectangle, Rounded Rectangle, Ellipse, Line and Button Shape tools to create either a new shape layer, or a filled shape. The techniques for using each tool are the same.

1 To draw a rectangle, oval, line or button shape choose the appropriate tool. Select either the Create New Shape layer button or the Create Filled Region button.

2 If you select the Create New Shape layer button, use the Options bar to create settings for the shape layer. You can use the Style pop-up to apply a pre-defined Layer Style to a shape layer. When you drag in the image window the shape automatically creates a new layer.

3 If you select the Create Filled Region button, the shape appears as a rasterized shape (a shape that consists of pixels) on the active layer. Select Fixed Size to create a shape to precise dimensions. Choose Anti-aliased (Ellipse and Rounded Rectangle) to help the object blend into its background by creating a slightly soft edge.

4 Position your cursor in the image window, then press and drag to create the shape. Release the mouse when the object is the required size. The object fills with the current foreground color.

5 To create a square or a circle, hold down Shift and drag with the Shape tool. Start to drag with a Shape tool, then hold down Alt/ option, to draw a shape from the center out.

The ImageReady Optimize Palette

The purpose of optimizing an image is to create an acceptable balance between image quality and download times.

The basic principles for optimizing images in ImageReady are the same as in Photoshop's Save for Web dialog box (see pages 192–193). The main difference is that the Original, Optimized, 2-Up and 4-Up tabs are part of the ImageReady window and therefore always available. The optimization settings and controls are located in the Optimize palette.

1 Choose Window>Optimize if the Optimize palette is not already showing.

2 Use the Preset pop-up menu to choose one of the pre-defined optimization settings. The Optimized image pane updates according to the settings you choose.

When you choose new optimization settings for the Optimized image pane, the remaining panes in 4-Up view do not update automatically. Choose Repopulate Views from the Optimize palette menu to repopulate the other panes with lower quality versions of those in the Optimized pane.

3 Use the 2-Up and 4-Up tabs to compare the visual quality of different optimization settings, along with file format, file size and download time readouts. To hide or show annotations in the 2-Up/4-Up views, choose View>Hide/Show Optimization Info.

4   In 4-Up view, select an optimized version of the image – a black highlight border appears around the selected pane. Choose Repopulate Views from the pop-up menu in the Optimize palette. The selected version now becomes the Optimized version and ImageReady automatically generates two smaller, lower-quality versions of the optimized image in the two remaining panes.

When you want to create custom optimization settings, click the expand/collapse triangle (▷) for Color Table, Dither, Transparency, Options (GIF and PNG-8), or Quality, Transparency, Options (JPEG and PNG-24). See pages 196–198 for further information on the options available:

5   When you begin working with optimization settings, use the pre-defined settings in the Preset pop-up as the basis for optimizing images.

6   To restore an optimized version of the image to the original version, first select the optimized version, then choose Original from the Preset pop-up menu.

7   If optimizing an image to a specific file size is more important than the resultant image quality, choose Optimize to File Size from the Optimize palette pop-up menu. Enter the required file size. Select the Auto Select GIF/JPEG option to allow ImageReady to choose the most effective compression format. Choose Current settings to use the current format as the basis for reducing the file size.

Saving an Optimized Image

After you decide on optimization settings that give you the correct balance between image quality and file size, you can then save an optimized version of the file.

If you are working on an optimized image in 2-Up or 4-Up view, when you choose File>Save Optimized As, the settings you apply to the image are those for the selected image pane.

1   If you are working with the Optimized tab selected, check that the current optimization settings in the Optimize palette are the ones you want. Then choose File>Save Optimized As.

2   If you are working in 2-Up view, make sure the Optimized pane is selected. If you are working with the 4-Up tab, make sure you select the pane with the settings you want to use for

optimizing the image. A selected pane is indicated by a black highlight border. Then choose File>Save Optimized As.

3   In the Save Optimized dialog box, specify a location and name for the file. The file format extension (e.g. .jpg) is appended automatically. Make sure you retain the file extension.

4   For the Save as Type pop-up menu, leave the Save Images option selected. Select the HTML and Images option if you want to save an additional HTML file that includes the image name, its dimensions in pixels and any other code necessary to display the image on a Web page. The HTML file is saved as a separate file with a .html extension in the specified folder. The image file is saved in an images folder that ImageReady creates automatically within the specified folder. This option is useful when saving images with slices (see Chapter 17.) Click the Save button.

Select Save Selected Slices from the Slices pop-up menu only when you have selected specific slices in the image prior to choosing the Save Optimized As command. ImageReady creates a complete HTML table capable of displaying the selected slices.

Animations and Rollovers

Animations are built from a series of GIF images which, when displayed in quick succession, create the illusion of movement. You create and control animations using the Animation and Layers palettes in ImageReady. Animations can be saved in GIF file format or exported to Macromedia® Flash® (SWF) format.

A rollover is an effect that is triggered by a mouse action. For example, a button may glow when the mouse cursor moves over it and then change shape in response to a mouse click.

Animations and rollovers can bring impact, movement and variety to a Web page, but they can also become distracting if not used carefully. Use these effects when they bring dynamism to a page and contribute to the message and content. Don't use animations and rollovers for their own sake.

Covers

Chapter Sixteen

Creating a Simple Animation

When you open or create an image in ImageReady, the image becomes the first frame in the Animation palette by default, even if you do not intend to create an animation.

Animations can range from the very simple to the very complex. Try to keep your animations simple at the outset. Remember that animation effects, if used indiscriminately on Web pages, can be distracting and as a result lose their intended impact.

1 Create an image in Photoshop, or directly in ImageReady as in this example. Use layers as the basis for the animation. The layers you create form the basic building blocks for the animation. Put elements you want to animate on separate layers.

To avoid confusion as you create an animation, make sure that you have created and finished editing all the objects and layers you want to use, before you start to build the animation.

2 Hide any layers containing elements you do not want to appear at the start of the animation.

3 Choose Window> Animation to show

the Animation palette if it is not already showing. Choose New Frame from the palette's pop-up menu, or click the New Frame button. This creates frame 2, which is a duplicate of the preceding frame.

Choose Window> Workspace> Interactivity Palette Locations to create a convenient arrangement of palettes for building animations and other web effects.

...cont'd

Animations are saved in the GIF file format. The JPEG and PNG formats cannot be used for animations.

When working in ImageReady, it is best to create and edit the animation in Original view. Options for editing animations are more limited in Optimized view.

Any changes you make on a layer that affect actual pixel values – for example, painting, changing color or tone, or using transform commands – will affect all frames in the animation in which the layer is present.

4 Make a change to a layer. Changes you make to the layers, such as layer visibility, position, opacity or layer effects, form the animation when the frames are viewed in quick succession. In this example the "P" is moved next to the "U".

5 Repeat Steps 3-4 as necessary. In this example, both the "P" and "U" are moved to the "S". Then, for the final frame, the "P", "U" and "S" are moved up to the "H".

6 Save the animation in Photoshop format as you build and make changes. This means you can return to the original file, if necessary, to make further adjustments. (See page 220 for information on saving an optimized version of the animation for use on the Web.)

Playing and Managing Frames

As you build an animation you will need to preview it and to control aspects such as looping and frame rate.

1   To play an animation, click the Play button. The animation plays in the image window and each frame in the Animation palette highlights in sequence as the animation plays. Click the Stop button to stop the animation at the current frame.

2   To select a frame, click on the frame in the Animation palette. The frame highlights and becomes the current frame. The current frame is displayed in the image window. It is the frame that can currently be edited.

3   To delete a frame, first click on it to select it. Then click the Wastebasket button at the bottom of the palette. Alternatively, drag the frame into the Wastebasket, or choose Delete Frame from the palette menu.

New Frame
Delete Frame
Delete Animation

4   To change the position of a frame, select the frame you want to move, then drag it to a new location. Release the mouse when you see a thick black bar at the position to which you want to move the frame.

5 To set the frame delay rate (the speed at which frames advance), first select a frame or multiple frames. Use the Frame Delay pop-up located below each frame. Either choose a value from the preset list, or choose Other then specify a delay in the Set Frame Delay dialog box.

Preview animations in a browser working live over the internet to get an accurate idea of the delay you specify.

| No delay |
| 0.1 seconds |
| 0.2 |
| 0.5 |
| 1.0 |
| 2.0 |
| 5.0 |
| 10.0 |
| Other... |
| ✓ 0 seconds |

Set Frame Delay

Set Delay: 2 seconds   [OK]
[Cancel]

6 To specify looping options, use the Loop pop-up in the bottom left corner of the Animation palette. Forever plays the animation in a continuous loop. Choose Other to specify a set number of times you want the animation to play. Enter a value in the Play ... times field.

| Once |
| ✓ Forever |
| Other... |

Set Loop Count

Play: 3 times   [OK]
[Cancel]

Copying and pasting frames

You can copy a frame or multiple frames and then paste the copied frame(s) into a new location in the current animation, or into a completely different animation.

1 To copy a frame, first select the frame. A black highlight indicates the frame is selected. Choose Copy Frame from the Animation palette menu.

2 Select a frame in which you want to paste the copied frame. Choose Paste Frame from the Animation palette menu. Choose an option for Paste Method then click OK.

Paste Frames

Paste Method
⦿ Replace Frames   [OK]
○ Paste Over Selection   [Cancel]
○ Paste Before Selection
○ Paste After Selection

☐ Link Added Layers

Animation

1	2	3	4	5	6	7	8
PUSH	PUSH	PUSH	PUSH	PUSH	PUSH	PUSH	PUSH
0 sec. *	0 sec. *	0 sec. *	2 sec. *	0 sec. *	0 sec. *	0 sec. *	2 sec. *

3 times ▾ ◄◄ ◄◀ ▶ ▶ ◧ ▣

Optimizing and Saving Animations

When you have created the frames for your animation and you are satisfied with the effect, you can optimize and then save the animation.

Continue to test other optimization settings and preview them until you are satisfied with the results.

1 To optimize an animation, click the Optimize tab in the ImageReady window. In the Optimize palette, choose the optimization settings you want to use from the Presets pop-up.

2 To preview the results of the optimization settings, choose File>Preview in, then choose from the list of available browsers. The browser launches and the animation plays in the browser window.

To export an animation to Flash (SWF) format, choose File>Export> Macromedia Flash (SWF). For a simple animation accept the default settings in the export dialog box, or create custom settings:

File format information and HTML code are displayed below the animation for information purposes. Close the browser.

3 To save the animation, choose File>Save Optimized As. Specify a location and a name for the file. Make sure you retain the .GIF file extension which should appear automatically.

4 Select the Save HTML file option to save the HTML code for the animation file. The HTML file is saved in the same folder and with the same name as the animation, but with a HTML file extension. Make sure you leave the Save Images option selected. Click the Save button.

OK the dialog box. Specify a location and name for the file. Open the animation in a browser to preview the result. ImageReady converts animation frames to SWF animation frames, but slice, image map and rollover settings are discarded.

Tweening

In ImageReady, the Tween command allows you to create smoother animations quickly and easily, by automatically creating additional frames between existing frames in the animation. These additional, in-between frames create smoother movement in the animation.

I To tween a frame, first click the New Frame button to create a duplicate of the first frame.

2 Make a change (for example, reposition an object) to the layer on which you are working.

3 Click the Tween button in the Animations palette, or choose Tween from the palette pop-up menu.

4 For Layers, select the Selected Layer option to vary only the currently selected layer in the selected frame, otherwise leave the option set to All Layers.

You can tween the last and first frames in an animation. This is useful to create a smooth transition from the end of an animation back to the beginning, when the animation is designed to loop a number of times.

5 Choose Parameter options to specify which elements you want to tween. In this example it is important to choose Position, as it is the position of the layers in the animation that varies. Select Opacity if opacity settings vary between frames. Select Effects if Layer Effects vary between frames.

Parameters
- ☑ Position
- ☑ Opacity
- ☑ Effects

6 Use the Tween with: pop-up to choose the frame with which you want to tween the currently selected frame.

Selection
First Frame
Previous Frame

7 Enter a value in the Frames to Add: field to specify the number of in-between frames. The more in-between frames you add, the smoother the animation, but the result is a larger file size.

8 OK the dialog box. The in-between frames are added as new frames. Subsequent frames are renumbered accordingly.

Animation

1	2	3	4	5	6	7	8	9	10

| 0 sec. ▾ | 0 sec. ▾ | 0 sec. ▾ | 0 sec. ▾ | 0 sec. ▾ | 0 sec. ▾ | 0 sec. ▾ | 0 sec. ▾ | 0 sec. ▾ | 0 sec. ▾ |

Forever ▾

Creating a Basic Rollover

A rollover image is an image whose appearance changes according to various mouse actions. For example, the image may change when the mouse cursor moves over it, or when it is clicked by the mouse. Rollover images are commonly used on Web pages and in multimedia interfaces. You use the Web Content palette together with the Layers palette to create rollover states for an image.

A rollover image can have a number of different states. The "Normal" state is the appearance of the image when it first loads in the browser window. The "Over" state is the state of the image when the mouse cursor moves over it.

A layer-based slice is indicated by a slice icon in the layers palette entry for that layer:

When you save an image with rollover states, each state is saved as a separate image. When you save the image with HTML coding, ImageReady automatically creates the JavaScript code necessary to display the rollover effects in a browser.

If you find the display of slices in the image window disconcerting, click the Slice Visibility button in the Toolbox:

1. Create the layers and any layer styles you will need for the rollover states in your image. Before you begin to build the rollover states, make sure you show only those layers that you want to be visible in the Normal state of the image.

2. In the Layers palette, select the layer whose contents you want to use to trigger the rollover effect.

3. In the Web Content palette, click the Create Layer-based Rollover button, or choose Create Layer-based rollover from the palette menu. This creates a layer-based slice for the contents of the selected layer and automatically creates the first rollover state – the Over state – as an entry below the layer-based slice entry.

4. Slices appear in the image window and a Slice tool icon (🔪) appears on the selected layer to indicate it is a layer-based slice.

5 Make sure you keep the Over state selected. Make changes to the Layers palette to represent the Over state of the image. This is the version of the image you want the viewer to see when they roll their cursor over the image. In this example, visibility for an outer glow layer effect is switched on for the layer.

Remember to click the Preview Document button to return to normal image editing mode when you have finished testing the rollover.

6 To check the result, click on the Normal and Over state entries in the Rollover palette in turn to see how the image in the image window changes. Or click the Preview Document button in the Toolbox, then move your cursor into the image window and over the rollover slices to see how the image responds.

7 To save the rollover for use in a Web page, choose File>Save Optimized As. Specify a folder and enter a name for the file. Choose HTML and Images from the Save As Type pop-up menu. When you click the Save button, ImageReady creates a HTML file together with the necessary JavaScript to display the rollover in a Web page. The individual images that make up the rollover are stored within an images folder within the specified folder.

8 You can open the HTML file in a browser to preview the results.

Slicing and Image Maps

Slicing allows you to create a single, complete image in Photoshop or ImageReady, then subdivide it into specific areas – the slices. ImageReady automatically generates the HTML code for a table that will hold the sliced image, or the code that will display the image using CSS (Cascading Style Sheets).

Using slices you can optimize parts of an image differently for different purposes; slices can become buttons and assigned links; and you can also create rollover states for slices. The functionality of slices varies slightly between Photoshop and ImageReady.

Use image maps to define areas of an image as clickable hypertext links in a Web page.

Covers

Chapter Seventeen

Slices from Guides & the Slice Tool

Slices are rectangular areas of an image that become the contents of a single cell in a HTML table, or that can be coded using Cascading Style Sheets. An image in ImageReady initially consists of a single slice by default, comprising the complete image. When you create a new slice, the remainder of the image is automatically divided into further slices.

You can create slices based on ruler guides or selections, or you can create a slice using the Slice tool. This section looks at techniques for creating slices from guides and using the Slice tool.

When you use the Create Slices from Guides command, ImageReady deletes previously created slices.

Slices from guides

1 Create or open an image. Drag in ruler guides to indicate where you want to create slices. (See page 23 for information

To create ruler guides, choose View>Rulers to show rulers along the top and left edge of the image window if they are not already showing. See page 23 for information on creating ruler guides.

on creating ruler guides.) Click the Edit in ImageReady button if you are not already working in ImageReady.

2 Choose Slices> Create Slices from Guides. The slices appear in the image. Each slice is

Slices you create using the Create Slices from Guides command and using the Slice tool are created as User-slices.

numbered. Slices created from guides are User-slices. (See page 229 for information on User- and Auto-slices.) A color adjustment, visible when slices are showing, is applied to slices to indicate User- and Auto-slices. (See page 229 for further information.)

...cont'd

Slices are rectangular areas of an image that become the contents of individual cells in a HTML table. When loaded in a browser, the image appears to be a single, composite image. In HTML terms, it is split into discreet, separate areas.

3 Choose the Slice Select tool (O), then click on a slice to select it. A colored bounding box appears around the slice, defining the area of the slice.

4 The selected slice also appears in the Slice palette. Choose Window>Slice if the palette is not already showing. Also, each slice in the image creates an entry in the Web Content palette.

The Slice tool

As soon as you select the Slice tool, existing slices display automatically.

1 To create a slice using the Slice tool, click on the tool to select it. Position your cursor on the image, then drag to define the area of the slice. The slice you define is a User-slice.

2 When you release the mouse, ImageReady automatically generates additional slices to enable the image to fit into a HTML table. The additional slices are Auto-slices.

"Smart" alignment guides appear as you draw and move slices in an image with multiple layers and/or existing slices, provided that Snap is selected in the View menu and Smart Guides is selected in the View>Show sub-menu. Use these interactive alignment guides to align slices accurately.

3 Hold down Shift as you drag with the Slice tool for a square slice. Hold down Alt/option and drag to create a slice from the center out.

4 Choose View>Snap to>Slices if you want the Slice tool to snap to other slices or guides. The snap takes effect when your cursor comes within 4 pixels of a slice or guide.

Creating Slices from Selections

You can also create slices from selections.

When you
click the Hide
Slices button
(Q), the color
adjustments
applied to slices disappears:

1 Create a
selection.
Choose
Select>
Create
Slice
from Selection. The
selection becomes a
User-slice. (See page
229 for information
on User and Auto-
slices.) The User-slice
is numbered and the
remainder of the image
is divided into further
slices as necessary

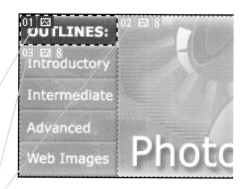

to fit the complete image into a HTML table, or for coding as
Cascading Style Sheets. The User-slice is selected and a highlight
bounding box appears around it. A color adjustment is applied
to the remainder of the image. This color adjustment is helpful in
distinguishing between User- and Auto-slices.

You cannot
create slices
from selections in
Photoshop.

If you create
a slice from
a feathered
selection, the
slice includes the
feathered area.

2 Continue creating slices as necessary. As you create additional
slices, slice numbers are updated. Slices are numbered from left to
right and top to bottom.

If you use a
non-rectangular
selection to
create a slice, the
slice itself covers
a rectangle that encompasses
the complete selection.

User- and Auto-slices

It can sometimes be less confusing to hide the display of Auto-slices. Select the Slice-select tool, then click the Hide/Show Auto Slices button in the Options bar:

Hide Auto Slices

You can promote an Auto-slice to a User-slice. In Photoshop select the Promote to User-slice option in the Options bar. In ImageReady choose Slices>Promote to User-slice.

The color adjustment applied to slices dims the brightness and contrast of unselected slices. This is for display purposes only. The color adjustment does not affect the final color of images.

User-slices have blue slice annotation symbols; Auto-slices have gray slice annotation symbols.

User-slices are indicated by a solid boundary line; Auto-slices by a dotted line.

A slice can have one of two statuses: User or Auto. There are more possibilities for modifying User-slices. Any slices you create (using guides, selections or the Slice tool) are User-slices. Slices created automatically by ImageReady to enable the remainder of the image to fit into a HTML table are Auto-slices. An image in ImageReady automatically consists of one Auto-slice comprising the full image.

You can change or "promote" an Auto-slice into a User-slice. User-slices can be assigned different optimization settings. Auto-slices in an image are initially linked and therefore share the same optimization settings. The link symbol which appears next to Auto-slices indicates that they share the same optimization settings.

There are two types of slices: Image or No Image. Image slices contain image information – pixels. No Image slices can contain a solid color, or HTML text. An Image slice is identified by the Image icon when slices are visible.

Starting in the top left corner, slices are numbered from left to right and top to bottom. As you add, delete and rearrange slices, slice numbers are updated automatically.

Different color adjustments on User- and Auto-slices and the slice information icons help you distinguish the two statuses. Unselected Auto-slices appear dimmer than unselected User-slices – the color adjustment on Auto-slices is twice as strong as that used to distinguish User-slices.

Working with Slices

Use the following techniques to hide and show slices and to select and deselect slices.

1 To hide slices and slice information such as slice number and slice type icons, click the Hide/Show Slice button (Q) in the Toolbox. To show slices, click the button again (Q).

2 To select a slice, select the Slice Select tool (O). Click on a slice. A colored bounding box with eight selection handles appears around the slice indicating it is selected. The color adjustment, which defines the area of the slices, is switched off for the selected slice.

3 To select multiple slices, select a slice, hold down Shift then click inside another slice to add it to the selection.

4 When you select a slice, it appears in the Slice palette. Choose Window>Slice to show the Slice palette if it is not already showing. Click the Expand button in the Slice tab, if necessary, to show all option categories for the slice, or click the Expand/Collapse triangle next to individual categories to show/hide specific areas of the palette. The default slice name and slice number appear in the Name entry box. (See page 232 for information on assigning URLs to slices so that they can function as buttons on a Web page.)

Photoshop and ImageReady can generate slices as a HTML table, or as Cascading Style Sheets. In the Save Optimized As dialog box (see page 194), click the Output settings button to specify which method is used.

To delete a User-slice, first select it then press the Backspace or Delete key. Auto-slices are automatically created to fill the same area.

In Photoshop, to hide/show slice numbers, use the Show Slice Numbers option in the Options bar.

You cannot move or resize User-slices in the Photoshop Save for Web dialog box.

To delete all User-slices, in Photoshop choose View>Clear Slices; in ImageReady choose Slices>Delete All.

5 Choose File>Preview in, then select a Browser from the sub-menu to preview the image in the browser window. The automatically generated HTML code

for the sliced image is also displayed in the browser window.

6 Use the Optimize palette to create optimization settings for the image. (See Chapter 15 for details). You can create different optimization settings for individual slices if required.

7 Choose Save Optimized As to save an optimized version of the image. (See page 214 for information on saving optimized images).

8 To move a slice, select the Slice Select tool, position your cursor within the slice you want to move then drag the slice.

9 To resize a slice, select the Slice Select tool. Select a slice then drag a side or corner resize handle.

Assigning URLs to Slices/Image Maps

You can make a slice or image map act as a clickable button that will link to another Web page by assigning a URL to the slice or image map area.

When you assign a URL to an Auto-slice it becomes a User-slice.

1 Select the Slice tool to select a slice. Select the Image Map Select tool to select an image map area. Click on a slice or image map to select it. Make sure the Slice or Image Map palette is showing. Details for the selected slice appears in the Slice palette. Information for a selected Image Map area appears in the Image Map palette.

With either the Slice or Slice Selection tool selected, hold down Ctrl/ Command to toggle temporarily to the other tool.

2 Slices and Image Map areas are automatically named. An underscore and a slice/image map number are added in the Name field.

3 Enter a URL in the URL entry field. You should include the http:// specifier at the beginning of the URL for absolute paths. You can also specify relative paths. You can choose any previously created URL from the URL pop-up menu.

4 If you are preparing images for a website that uses frames, specify a target frame – where the HTML file you link to will appear – using the Target entry field. Enter the name of the target frame exactly as defined in the frameset file.

Image Maps

The Image Map tools and palette allow you to create areas in an image that become clickable hyperlinks when the image is used in a HTML file. Unlike slicing an image, where individual slices become separate files, creating an image map keeps the image as a single file, with areas of the image defined as links. As well as rectangular areas, image maps enable you to create circular and irregular areas to act as links.

1 To create an image map, select one of the Image Map tools. Press and drag diagonally to create rectangular or oval image map areas. For the Polygon Image Map tool, position your cursor on the image, click, move the cursor to a new position (do not click and drag), then click again. Repeat this process to create the irregular shape you require. Click back at the start point to close the shape. You can also double-click to close the shape.

HOT TIP *With the Rectangular Image Map tool selected, hold down Shift to create a square image map region.*

HOT TIP *"Smart" alignment guides appear as you draw and move image map areas in an image with multiple layers and/or existing image map areas, provided that Snap is selected in the View menu and Smart Guides is selected in the View>Show sub-menu. Use these interactive alignment guides to align image maps accurately.*

2 To show existing image map areas in an image, select the Image Map Select tool, or choose View> Show>Image Maps. You can also click the Image Map Visibility button ( ) in the Toolbox to show/hide image map areas in the image window.

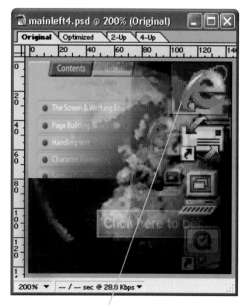

3 Use the Image Map Select tool to select areas of an image map. Click in an image map area to select it.

4   To reposition an image map
     area, position the Image Map
     Select tool in the area, then
     press and drag the area in the
     image window.

5   To resize a selected image map
     area, position the Select cursor
     on one of the resize handles
     on the area's border, then press
     and drag.

6   You can also control
     the size and position
     of a selected image
     map area in the
     Dimensions section of
     the Image Map palette.

Slice	Table	⬍ Image Map	▸
Name:	ImageMap_03		
URL:	http:www.robshuff.co.uk		⌄
Target:			⌄
Alt:			

▽ **Dimensions**

X: 125   Radius: 18
Y: 86

7   To delete an image
     map area, select
     it then press the
     Backspace or Delete key.

Index

N

O

M

P